THE LAKOTA WAY

Joseph M. Marshall III was born on the Rosebud Indian Reservation in what is now south-central South Dakota. Marshall was raised by his maternal grandparents and his first language is Lakota. He is a historian, educator, and speaker, and he has been a technical adviser and actor in television movies, including *Return to Lonesome Dove*. A recipient of the Wyoming Humanities Award, he is the author of two collections of essays, *On Behalf of the Wolf and the First Peoples* and *The Dance House*, and a novel, *Winter of the Holy Iron*. He lives in Jackson Hole, Wyoming. For more information about Joseph Marshall, please visit *www.thunderdreamers.com*.

Praise for
The Lakota Way: Stories and Lessons for Living

"It is rare to find a storyteller who is also a natural healer; a person concerned not just with the excitement a story might generate, but also carrying deep intuitions about how each story has a teaching essence enfolded in it. With gentle humor and fierce beliefs about conduct of life, Joseph Marshall places his personal and magical words just so into the human heart, reminding us all through the stirring of memory, that full capacity and beauty are still in each soul presently and irrevocably so. To cause memory; that has always been the real work of stories."
—Clarissa Pinkola Estés, Ph.D., author of *Women Who Run With the Wolves* and *La Curandera*

"A book of virtues, Sioux style, that puts the work of Allan Bloom and William Bennett to shame. Wise words by an authentic representative of Lakota culture . . . add up to an inspirational book of a high order."
—*Kirkus Reviews*

"This is a Native Book of Virtues . . . Joe Marshall opens the tipi flap and invites us all to enter, to enjoy customary Lakota hospitality, to listen and to learn. Will we have the wisdom this time to enter and sit quietly while the elders tell us their stories?"
—Roger Welsch, author of *Old Tractors Never Die*

"Marshall beautifully imparts Lakota wisdom . . . he certainly knows how to weave a story. An inspiring guide for a wide audience."
—*Library Journal*

The Lakota Way

Stories and Lessons for Living

Joseph M. Marshall III

Penguin Compass

PENGUIN COMPASS
Published by the Penguin Group
Penguin Group (USA) Inc., 375 Hudson Street,
New York, New York 10014, U.S.A.
Penguin Group (Canada), 90 Eglinton Avenue East, Suite 700, Toronto, Ontario,
Canada M4P 2Y3 (a division of Pearson Penguin Canada Inc.)
Penguin Books Ltd, 80 Strand, London WC2R 0RL, England
Penguin Ireland, 25 St Stephen's Green, Dublin 2, Ireland
(a division of Penguin Books Ltd)
Penguin Group (Australia), 250 Camberwell Road, Camberwell, Victoria 3124,
Australia (a division of Pearson Australia Group Pty Ltd)
Penguin Books India Pvt Ltd, 11 Community Centre, Panchsheel Park,
New Delhi – 110 017, India
Penguin Group (NZ), 67 Apollo Drive, Rosedale, North Shore 0632,
New Zealand (a division of Pearson New Zealand Ltd)
Penguin Books (South Africa) (Pty) Ltd, 24 Sturdee Avenue, Rosebank,
Johannesburg 2196, South Africa

Penguin Books Ltd, Registered Offices: 80 Strand, London WC2R 0RL, England

First published in the United States of America by Viking Compass,
a member of Penguin Putnam Inc. 2001
Published in Penguin Compass 2002

50th Printing

THE LIBRARY OF CONGRESS HAS CATALOGED
THE HARDCOVER EDITION AS FOLLOWS:
Marshall, Joseph, 1945–
The Lakota way : stories and lessons from living / Joseph Marshall.
p. cm.
Includes index.
ISBN 0-670-89456-7 (hc.)
ISBN 978-0-14-219609-0 (pbk.)
1. Teton Indians—Folklore. 2. Values—Great Plains.
3. Tales—Great Plains. I. Title
E99.T34 M37 2001
398.2'089'9752—dc21   2001035225

Printed in the United States of America
Set in Simoncini Garamond
Designed by Nancy Resnick

Contents

Introduction:
Let the Wind Blow Through You

A playground dispute in the fourth grade concluded with a barrage of epithets hurled at me, each one more stinging than the one before. I was called every derogatory name for Indians that two white fourth-grade classmates could remember. Stunned, I could think of nothing equally hurtful to throw back.

That evening, still hurting from the insults, I told my grandfather about the incident.

"Words can hurt," he said, "but only if you let them. They called you bad names. Were you changed into the things they called you?"

"No," I replied.

"You cannot forget what they said any more than you cannot feel the wind when it blows. But if you learn to let the wind blow through you, you will take away its power to blow you down. If you let the words pass through you, without letting them catch on your anger or pride, you will not feel them."

My grandfather's wise counsel has helped me through many storms in life. How his quiet, yet powerful comments influenced me, and still do, is one of my favorite stories. When I tell young people how my grandfather's words helped me, I can feel those words going into their hearts.

Stories and storytelling were all around me in my childhood. The storytellers were my Lakota grandparents—both maternal and paternal—and others of their generation. Strangely enough, these elders didn't seem old to me, but I did have a sense that they'd been around a long time and knew everything.

If the storytellers were old, their stories were much older. The Grandmas and Grandpas were the living repositories for all those wonderful stories told them by their elders from generations before. The stories I heard and learned provide lessons that I can apply in the present; but they also connect me to the past—to a way of life that has endured far longer than I can imagine—and to the people who walked the land and left old trails to follow. And because I and others like me were, and are, hearing and remembering the stories, that way of life will remain viable through us.

I never tired of the stories, and I would ask to hear my favorites again and again, my version of watching a movie over and over. Those stories were not just of humans, or "two-leggeds," they were about other kinds of people as well: the elk people, the bear people, the bird people, and so on. And they were about the land. I never heard a story that didn't involve the land in some way.

Everything in those stories is equally alive and able to affect everything else. A winter storm, for example, could have a personality; it could be impatient, pushy, broad shouldered. A cottonwood sapling could whine and argue; the summer wind could be persuasive, enticing all the blades of grass to bend and sway in the same direction at the same moment. These mechanisms in Lakota storytelling exist because the storytellers believe all things are related. I therefore look at winter storm clouds gathering or feel the wind on my face and feel connected to them. I don't regard them as something merely to plague two-leggeds.

Stories entertained and informed, but, of course, that was only their obvious purpose. Tales and allegories told by Lakota elders very directly enabled an entire culture to survive because they carried the culture within them. The stories I learned growing up were consciously told again and again to teach me about life—my purpose in it and my path through it. These stories are certainly not random; each illustrates a virtue that, within Lakota culture, is essential to balance and happiness.

To the Lakota, virtues such as humility, respect, sacrifice, and honesty carry a different weight and substance than they do in western culture. For us these qualities are not so much elusive goals as they are essential parts of everyday life. They are instilled in us as firmly and as specifically as American courtesies like saying "please" and "thank you," or "bless you" after someone sneezes.

I knew growing up that at some point I was supposed to be the things I learned in the stories: compassionate, honorable, and brave, and so forth. I knew this because the storytellers lived the lessons they imparted in their stories, and they practiced what they preached: They were compassionate, they were honorable, and they were brave and wise.

The virtues espoused by the stories in this book were and are the foundation and moral sustenance of Lakota culture. There is nothing more important. It isn't that we don't care about physical comfort or material possessions, it is because we don't measure ourselves or others by those things. We believe we are measured by how well, or how little, we manifest virtue in our life's journey.

When life for us was forever altered by the arrival of Europeans—when entire populations were devastated by disease, alcohol, war, and dispossession—we survived by living by the virtues we learned from our stories. We relied on being the kind of people our stories told us our ancestors had been, and thereby we remained true to ourselves and to them, and we are still surviving.

By providing both knowledge and inspiration, stories continue to strengthen Lakota society and enable us to cope with our world and the times we live in. Stories of virtue are at the core of cultural renewal for each new generation. But even more importantly they reach us individually as men and women, young and old.

The stories herein are intended to provide an experiential insight into our tradition, customs, and values. Throughout the ages they have been the lessons that have shaped and transformed our lives, and they still have the power to do so. If you are not careful, they may do that for you. While they will not turn the non-Lakota into a Lakota, they have much to offer anyone who is curious about life. They are our gift to the world, if you will. They rise out of our triumphs, our defeats, our strengths, and our weaknesses. They are not guarded secrets; they are markers on the road of life—the answers soaring across the open prairies of our lives on the winds of wisdom—helping us, perhaps helping you. That, at least, is my prayer.

I, for one, am always ready and willing to recall and retell the stories I have heard. Especially when the wind blows.

Joseph M. Marshall III
Sicangu Oglala Lakota

The Lakota Way

Humility

✛ The Story of No Moccasins

Among us the old ones are the best models for how we should live our lives. Every old person is a collection of stories because of all that each one has seen and lived and all that happens in the world around them in a lifetime. I have not met an old person yet who was not a strong exemplar of at least one virtue, and many are outstanding exemplars of more than one.

Such a person was an old woman named No Moccasins. She lived in a time before the coming of the horses (prior to 1700).

No Moccasins and her husband, Three Horns, had lived long lives. They had a son and a daughter and several grandchildren. No Moccasins, in fact, was grandmother to all the children in the village. She was a small woman, and by her sixty-seventh winter her hair was the color of new-fallen snow. The lines in her face seemed to show the many trails she had walked in her life. No visitor to her modest but orderly lodge ever left hungry, and rarely without a gift in hand, something that was finely quilled. She was known far and wide for her intricate quilling patterns and designs, and many women came to learn her skill.

But in spite of all of that she was known mainly as the wife of Three Horns.

Three Horns was a man of excellent reputation. He had been a warrior far past the time when most men lost the strength of arm and leg as well as the will to take risks. So in his lifetime he had collected many, many war honors. The lance to which his eagle feathers were tied was twice as long as a man was tall. Every feather was an honor, of course, and no other man could boast of such a thing. When he finally turned from the warpath, he took his place on the council of elders. There he offered his wisdom unselfishly and the skill with which he spoke could not be matched. He was seventy winters old, but his appearance could take the breath away. He didn't have the big belly that many old men did. He stood straight and tall, and his hair, which hung to his waist, was silvery white.

In the village everyone turned to Three Horns for advice. It seemed as though he had always been there. So when he fell ill and took to his deathbed, the entire village was in disbelief.

Word traveled fast and soon many, many people from other villages came to pay honor to the dying leader. Three Horns' tiny village grew to twice its size in a matter of days. No Moccasins, her daughter, and several other women were kept busy cooking to feed all the guests. When Three Horns was told about all the people who had come, he asked the oldest people in the gathering to come to his lodge.

The four men and two women who came to No Moccasins and Three Horns' lodge saw in the man's half of the lodge, which was to the north, the long eagle-feather staff, bows and arrows and lances, and buffalo-hide shields that were the colorful symbols of the glorious life of a warrior. Three Horns, weak from his illness, spoke in a low voice with No Moccasins, who was sitting beside him. But he seemed to grow stronger as he went on. No Moccasins, as she had always done, saw to the comfort of her guests and her husband and remained respectfully quiet.

"My friends and relatives," he began, "thank you for coming into our lodge. I have been honored to share this lodge with my wife for nearly fifty winters. In that time we were given a fine son and a fine daughter and many grandchildren. Our people saw difficulty as well as good. We took to the path of war now and then and good men were hurt or died. We are feared and respected by our enemies. The number of our lodges and villages has grown in that time. We are a strong people; our ways are good. I am thankful to the Great Mystery for bringing me into this world as a Lakota! I have lived a good life and I am ready for the next. Before I leave I have a story to tell, and I ask that after the sun comes up tomorrow you tell this same story to all the people gathered here. That is why I have asked you to come today. Here is what I want you to know.

"When I was a young man I traveled south from my mother and father's village to hunt. I came to a village that was encamped for the summer just north of the Running Water River. There was great feasting and a dance at that time, for there had been a fight and a great victory over enemies to the south. I was invited to join the celebration. It was a good time. There was much food and we danced far into the night.

"I awoke the next morning beside the trail to the water and looked into the largest and most wonderful eyes I had ever seen. A young woman was gazing down at me. She said, 'It is funny what suddenly grows beside this trail.' I jumped to my feet and followed her to the water and carried the water skins back to the village for her. That was the best chore I have ever done in my life.

"The next evening I stood in line outside the lodge of this young woman, with all the other young men who had come to court her. Her name was Carries the Fire and she did put the fire in my heart. I was very surprised when she asked me to come again the next evening. You will not be surprised when I tell you I remained in her village until the autumn hunts. By then, for reasons I still cannot understand but for which I am grateful, she had decided that I might be a good husband. So I went back north to tell my family so they could prepare the gifts to her family for the bride price.

"We were married the following spring. In between was the longest winter of my life. So I left my family and became a part of her village, as is a custom among us. Not long after that, enemies came among us from the south on a revenge raid for the defeat they had suffered before. They killed a man and took two young women. A war party went south on their trail. I went along.

"We trailed them for a half a moon, it seemed, going far into country I had never seen. We traveled fast and caught up with them as they rejoined their village. We hid and watched. We saw where they had put the two young women. Later we saw where their night sentinels were and made a plan.

"There were six of us. That night two of us would set a fire to the east of the village, and two of us would do the same to the west. While the men of the village were busy putting out the fires, two of us would sneak in and take back our young women. The plan worked, except for one thing: I was one of the two who sneaked into the village, and I was captured.

"By dawn all of our war party had escaped back to the north with the two young women, and I was glad to pay the price of a good raid. As you might think, my captors were very angry. They made me a slave. All my clothing was taken from me—everything. I was led around naked; everyone laughed. I was made to work. I pulled drag poles like a dog until my hands and knees were bleeding. They teased me; they threw dirt in my face. Women pulled up their dresses in front of me and laughed, showing me that I was no longer a man. They gave me no food so I had to fight with the dogs for scraps. At night they bound me hand and foot and stretched me between two stout poles. There was no way to escape. I began to feel lower than a dung beetle.

"I lost count of the days, but I looked for ways to escape. But lack of food made me very weak, and I knew that before I was too weak I had to escape. After a time they stopped putting a guard to sit and watch me at night. Night after night I pulled at the poles which held me, and little by little I loosened them. But someone saw what I had done and pounded the poles in deeper. I was discouraged.

"I am not ashamed to tell you that one night I prayed to the Great Mystery to give me a quick death. I could not escape; I was too weak.

"One night it was cold and rainy, and I was naked and shivering. There was no one about; it was too cold. Even the dogs curled up out of the rain. My heart was sad as I thought about my young wife and that I would never, ever see her again. I thought about her so much that her face appeared to me. After a moment I realized it was real; she was there! While I lay there in disbelief she cut my bonds with her knife, pulled me to my feet, and guided me out of the enemy's village.

"I was weak from hunger and my mind was not clear. But I know we walked through the night and by dawn we arrived at a hiding place she had prepared. The rain had fallen through the night and washed out our tracks. She could not have found a better time to come.

"She had hidden food and weapons. As my mind cleared I saw that she was wearing men's clothes—mine—to disguise herself for the journey. We hid, and we ate and rested. She told me that the other men had returned home with the news that I had been killed . She grieved for a time, she said, but she found herself not believing I was really dead. One night she made preparations and left the camp. The others had told her where the enemy camp was located. She knew where to look. After many days of hiding and watching she came into the camp on that rainy night.

"Though our tracks were washed out by the rain, the enemy knew we had to travel north to come home. So they sent out a war party.

"After a few days of resting and hiding we were eager to start home. We knew to be cautious, of course, and we looked often at our back trail. That is how we saw others heading in the same direction: six of them moving fast. I knew they had to be from the village where I had been a captive and that those six men were the best of their warriors. I had escaped when they were certain I could not. They could not know that I had help. Because my escape was an insult they could not let pass, they sent out their best trackers, their fiercest warriors.

"We covered our trail as best we could but it did not matter. They were running, and I could not. Carries the Fire and I decided that we should hide so that we would not leave a trail they could find. But they had to be thrown off somehow. I thought about that but I could do nothing, so I did not speak that thought to her. But she had thought the same.

"We made a good hiding place in an old bear's den. That afternoon while I slept she slipped away. She returned that evening, wet and barefoot. She had placed her moccasins near a creek to lay a false trail for our pursuers. Later she told me that when they nearly spotted her, she hid in a beaver's lodge. She had to go into the creek and come up inside the beaver's house. I teased her, saying that she should have a new name—No Moccasins.

"After two days we left our hiding place and struck out west and traveled in that direction for three days, then north. I began to call her No Moccasins because it was a name of honor for what she had done. That is why my wife is called No Moccasins. Though I grew stronger each day it was not an easy journey home. We had to watch for enemies, find food, and a shelter each night. But it was her quiet courage, more than anything, that was our greatest strength.

"The people were surprised to see us. They believed that I had been killed and that my wife had gone off and killed herself. That is not unknown. My wife did not want me to tell our story and would only let me say that I had escaped from my captors. The people honored me for that, but it was not my victory.

"I have asked you old ones to our lodge to witness for me. It is time to repay the great debt I owe my wife. Throughout my life I was fortunate as a warrior and somehow I was able to win some honors and gain a reputation. Yet all those honors are not mine because I could not have achieved them if my wife had not risked her life. I have not heard of any man in my lifetime who has done a braver deed. She traveled alone into enemy country and sneaked into an enemy's village. Few men can say they have done that.

"Because of her deed I took to the warpath each time with one thought in mind: to be worthy of my wife. For my life long I have tried to be worthy, but I am afraid I am not. So I must give all these honors to the one who truly deserves them. I give them to my wife. I ask that my warrior weapons and my eagle-feather staff be moved from the man's place in our lodge to the woman's place, where they rightfully should be.

"I will leave this world soon and I ask that another thing be done. I ask that my burial scaffold hold only my body wrapped in my burial robe. I will leave this world as the man I was before I met my wife: poor and unadorned. All that I appeared to be would not have been if not for this woman."

Three Horns sighed deeply and settled back. No Moccasins silently wiped away her tears and pulled a robe up over her husband.

"I have known good people in my life," Three Horns continued. "Many were wise, honorable, generous, and brave. But none, except this old woman who sits beside me as always, had the one strength that gives true meaning to all the others— humility.

"She did a brave thing, and no one—not the strongest warrior among us—has yet to do the same. Yet she cared not if anyone ever knew. It is time that everyone knows. Thus I have spoken."

The old ones who gathered with Three Horns gave their word to tell the story of No Moccasins' courage and humility. Through the days and nights that followed, young and old alike crowded around the campfires to listen to those old ones. Before long No Moccasins' name rose with the smoke from many campfires.

Days later Three Horns died in the arms of his beloved No Moccasins. Though her loss was great she comforted others. As he wished, Three Horns' burial scaffold was unadorned. Those who mourned for him also honored his widow.

No Moccasins cut her hair short in mourning, but nothing else outwardly changed. She lived her life the same as always—a small, quiet old woman amidst the bustle of a busy village. She gave her husband's eagle-feather staff, his shield, and his weapons to the Kit Fox Warrior Society. They, in turn, decided to hang those symbols of honor in the great council lodge in the very center of the village. There they would remain as a reminder of one man's courage and an old woman's humility.

The honor and reverence that Three Horns was given in his life now belonged to No Moccasins. Not a day went by that a gift of food was not left outside her lodge door, and every day she shared those gifts with the very young and the very old. For the rest of her days No Moccasin wanted for nothing. In the winter the firewood piled outside her door was nearly as high as the lodge. This, too, she shared. She welcomed all who came to visit, and many who did were warriors from near and far. They came to bring gifts and to share a meal, and to sit in the presence of courage to learn humility.

No Moccasins died in her seventieth winter. On her burial scaffold were hung her husband's shield, his weapons, and the eagle-feather staff. On the ground below were piled hundreds of moccasins so she would not have to journey to the other side in bare feet.

The Quiet Path

Lakota tradition encouraged its fighting men to publicly recount their exploits in battle. *Waktoglaka (wah-kto-glah-kah)* is the word for that old custom, meaning "to tell of one's victories." It seems illogical that a culture in which humility was a virtue could allow its fighting men to brag in public. There was, however, an essential requirement: Each and every action recounted had to be verified by at least one witness. That verification ensured the truth. To truthfully describe one's action in combat through the forum of ceremony was not considered bragging because the recounting—the story of the action—was a gift. It became part of the identity and the lore of the storyteller's warrior society, and it served to strengthen the entire village—not to mention that the deed recounted served as an example for young men to emulate.

Most men who did the *waktoglaka* did not repeat the story unless asked because they realized the value of humility. While exploits in the arena of combat were the way to establish and enhance a good reputation and gain status in the community, lack of appropriate humility was a sure way to taint one's reputation and erode hard-won status. In other words, once the battle was over it was time to be humble.

To traditional Lakota, humility was the one virtue that enhanced other virtues. To be generous was good, for example, as long as one did not call attention to his or her generosity. Anything good that was done or said with humility carried more impact. According to all the stories, one of the most humble of all Lakota was Crazy Horse.

Crazy Horse was an Oglala Lakota. The Oglala, which means "to scatter one's own," were (and are) one of the seven Lakota groups. His is one of the most familiar names to emerge from the turbulent nineteenth century in the American West. In western American history, written by Euro-Americans, he is popularly regarded as the conqueror of both General George Crook and Lieutenant Colonel George Custer. On June 17, 1876, he led seven hundred to nine hundred Lakota and Cheyenne warriors and stopped Crook's northward advance at the Battle of the Rosebud, on the Rosebud River in what is now north central Wyoming. Eight days later, one thousand to twelve hundred Lakota and Northern Cheyenne warriors under his leadership, as well as the able leadership of several other notable Lakota battlefield leaders, defeated Custer's Seventh Cavalry at the Battle of the Little Bighorn. Crazy Horse was thirty-six years old at the time, and his combat experience and leadership helped to thwart—albeit temporarily—the United States Army's grand plan of 1876 to capture and herd all the Lakota onto reservations once and for all. But we Lakota don't remember him primarily because he defeated Crook or Custer; we remember him because—in spite of his larger-than-life achievements on the field of battle—he was a humble man.

Crazy Horse was born to be a warrior and a leader. He had an ability to stay calm in the midst of chaos and confusion, and to lead by example. In the Lakota society of his day the arena of combat provided opportunities for fighting men to display skill and courage. Acts of bravery on the battlefield earned them honors within their warrior societies and status in the society at large. Many men who achieved a following as combat leaders also went on to become political leaders as well, such as the Hunkpapa Lakota Sitting Bull.

As a matter of fact, Crazy Horse's steadiness under fire earned him his first adult name, prior to Crazy Horse. Because he had a habit of dismounting in the midst of fighting, then kneeling beside his war horse to take deliberate aim at the enemy, he became known as His Horse Stands in Sight. Such conduct earned him more combat honors by his early twenties than most men achieved in an entire lifetime. He was known far and wide for his daring and recklessness in combat, but also for his ability to make good tactical decisions. If anyone earned the right to participate in the waktoglaka ceremony, it was he. But according to all the stories handed down about him, he never did.

For all of his life Crazy Horse was painfully shy and probably spoke in public only twice. Though he was entitled to wear the symbols of his many achievements on the battlefield—eagle feathers—he was known to dress plainly. If he wore any decoration, at all it was usually a single feather.

His refusal to do what was expected of all accomplished warriors—recount his exploits in combat—raised more than a few eyebrows because he was bucking tradition, but it also endeared him to many. Those exploits are the basis for the legend of Crazy Horse; but, sadly, they overshadow the real man—the man, the stories say, who would walk through camp with his head down in humility when he had every right to strut with arrogance. To the Lakota who knew, loved, and admired him, his humility only enhanced his achievements and he didn't need to recount his exploits. Many, many others did it for him.

Crazy Horse didn't ask or volunteer to be a leader. His reputation brought men to him, especially during that critical period following the Battle of the Little Bighorn when the U.S. Army stepped up its campaign against him. Because of his reputation and the humility with which he always conducted himself, just over nine hundred people followed him. Only a few more than a hundred were fighting men. The rest were old people and women and children, and they all endured hardship and uncertainty. But all of the fighting men and most, if not all, of the others would have continued to fight against the whites to the last man, or woman, or child if Crazy Horse had chosen that as the best course of action. But he chose otherwise. As a true testament of their loyalty, Crazy Horse's people followed him into an uncertain future when—for the welfare of his noncombatants—he finally surrendered to the United States. He was the last Lakota leader to do so.

Without a doubt people followed Crazy Horse because of his courage as a fighting man and his ability as a military and civilian leader. We Lakota will always remember him for those very reasons. As a Sicangu/Oglala Lakota I will always admire him for those achievements, but I will likewise never forget that he was a humble man. For me, his humility outshines his fame.

Humility was a virtue that the Lakota of old expected their leaders to possess. A quiet, humble person, we believed, was aware of other people and other things. An arrogant, boastful man was only aware of himself. Interestingly, our methods of selecting leaders today seem to favor the arrogant and boastful.

The process that we, as a nation, endure every four years is the same that many Native American tribes, or nations seem to mimic on a more frequent basis. In Lakota society of the not-too-distant past, however, it was the people who approached the man who possessed the qualities of leadership. One of those qualities was humility.

If humility was a virtue important for everyone to practice, it was absolutely necessary for a leader. Humility can provide clarity where arrogance makes a cloud. The last thing the people wanted was someone whose judgment and actions were clouded by arrogance. Several years ago I watched my uncle, then president of the Rosebud Sioux Tribe, diffuse a volatile moment with simple humility. A woman walked into his office and proceeded to ridicule and berate him, insulting him in every way she could think of because she or her family had been denied a service by one of the tribal service agencies. He didn't interrupt her; he waited until she finished her tirade. Then, instead of taking umbrage because he, and the office he held, had been grievously insulted, he, with his head down, quietly and respectfully replied, "Yes, that is why I have this job. So you can insult me when something goes wrong. Thank you for telling me your problem." The woman could only walk away. She had expected her words to be met with anger because an arrogant person would have reacted in that manner. When there was no anger, no arrogant retort, she didn't know how to handle the humility.

Now the process of selecting leaders apparently leaves no room for humility: A man or a woman who believes he or she can be a leader approaches the people by declaring *candidacy*. In most cases the candidate is not known to the people and consequently is forced to do at least a little boasting, and certainly a lot of promising. To make matters worse we are besieged by more than one candidate. This all brings to mind the story of *Iktomi,* the Trickster.

Iktomi was hungry as usual. In fact he couldn't remember when he had last eaten. So without a solid plan in mind he set about to feed himself. Circumstances were not favorable for a quick meal, however, since Iktomi was not a good hunter. As a matter of fact, he was the worst hunter around. He was not proficient with weapons and he was very slow of foot. Strangely, though, he was confident because he knew he was one of the trickiest beings to walk the Earth.

He came upon a trail and followed it. One never knew where such trails could lead, but of one thing he was certain: Chances were it would lead to opportunity. And opportunity was the key to Iktomi's survival. He gained the crest of hill and as he started down he saw someone coming up the hill. It was *Mato,* the bear.

Iktomi hid immediately. Except for *Tatanka,* the bison, Mato was the most powerful creature on four legs. One swipe of his paw could send skinny little Iktomi into the next world, and it was a place Iktomi was not anxious to go. From the middle of a plum thicket Iktomi watched as Mato lumbered up the hill. Iktomi suddenly realized that he was sitting in the middle of ripe plums, a favorite food for Mato. He was on the verge of panic and about to run for his very life when he saw that Mato was covered with scars from many old wounds. An idea formed in his opportunistic little brain.

Leaving the thicket he went back down the trail and began to whistle as he walked. Mato took immediate notice, of course, but because of his poor eyesight he had to wait to see what was making such a cheerful noise.

"It's you!" he growled as Iktomi stopped. "Get out of my way! I have to find food to fatten up for the winter. Go away unless you want me to eat you!"

Iktomi's knees were knocking and his heart was pounding. But he had a plan and it wouldn't work if Mato saw that he was terrified.

"Greetings, brother Mato!" Iktomi called out in the loudest, bravest voice he could muster. "It's good to see you, but you must step aside because I am in a hurry!"

Mato was astonished. He had never known anyone to face him. All the two-leggeds ran away at his approach. Now this skinny little being was telling him to step aside.

"I hope you taste much better than you look!" Mato said. "Don't say I didn't warn you! Beings much more powerful than you tremble at the sight of me!"

"That is true," replied Iktomi, "but you don't know how powerful I truly am."

"The only thing powerful about you is your odor!" roared Mato, so incensed at Iktomi's arrogance that he rose on his hind legs.

There are few sights more frightening than Mato, on his hind legs, rising to a height equal to four of Iktomi's, whose insides were turning to mush. It was much too late to run because the only thing on the prairie that could outrun Mato was Tatanka. Iktomi gathered all his courage, which he never had in abundance, and stood his ground.

"I am more powerful than you!" he retorted. "And unless you are too afraid I can prove it to you!"

Mato crashed to the Earth, doubled up in laughter. His loud guffaws rolled across the hills as he howled with laughter until the tears ran from his beady little eyes. When he could laugh no longer he sat up and stared at Iktomi, who, of course, was the very image of confidence.

"There is no one more powerful than me," said Mato. "Therefore I am afraid of nothing, not even you!" At that he rolled over with laughter once again. "So," he giggled, "prove to me how powerful you are!"

"I will," said Iktomi, "but I will give you first chance. For not only am I powerful, I am also fair."

Mato giggled all the more. "What must I do?"

"I know you have been wounded many, many times and you are still alive."

"Yes," admitted Mato. "I have been wounded many times by two-leggeds, so I have many arrowheads and lance points in my body."

"Exactly!" shouted Iktomi, "but so do I, and much more than you. Still, I will give you a chance. You must cough up all the arrowheads and lance points in your body and I will do the same. Then we shall see who has more."

Mato couldn't stop giggling. "Very well," he said, "I will, but it hardly seems worth the trouble. I could just eat you and be done with it."

"Then we need to make a wager," Iktomi said. "If you win, I will show you a creek where the fish are so plentiful you can catch them with your eyes closed. What's more, you can eat me, too. If I win, you must provide me with food for a month."

"You probably are stringy and would be tough to eat, but you have a wager nonetheless," decided Mato. "I'll go first."

So saying, he jumped to his feet, rose to his hind legs, and began to pound his chest and then coughed and coughed until he began to spit up arrowheads and lance points. Of course, as Iktomi knew he would have to, Mato closed his eyes as he gagged and coughed. And as the objects flying out of him were beginning to form a large pile, Iktomi sprang into action. As quickly as Mato coughed up arrowheads and lance points, he swallowed them. When Mato finally finished and sat back down, he looked at the pile in front of him. It was rather small.

"Now you," he said, not the least bit worried. He knew

Iktomi's puny little body couldn't possibly have more than one or two arrowheads.

Iktomi raised himself as tall as he could stand, pounded on his chest and began to cough and cough. Soon one arrowhead came out, then another, then a lance point. In front of the astonished Mato, Iktomi's pile grew and grew, higher and higher. It was hard to believe that Iktomi could have been wounded so many times, but there it was, a pile of arrowheads and lance points much larger than Mato's.

If Mato was dimwitted, he was also honorable, so he yielded, though he kept mumbling to himself in astonishment. And true to his word he supplied Iktomi with berries and fish for an entire month.

Our current method of choosing leaders reminds me too much of Mato's loss at the hands of the clever Iktomi. And although that system functions primarily to perpetuate itself, we shouldn't be prevented from realistically assessing the true character of any candidate. Records of achievement are important—if they are real and not concocted, like Iktomi's—but so are character and virtue. I am always leery of anyone who first and foremost touts his or her record of public service. I tend to look at the person. What is he or she without that record? I look for the No Moccasins and the Crazy Horses because I am influenced by quiet dignity and the person who walks through camp with his or her head down, rather than the one who struts. I would vote for a truly humble person.

Humility may be the most difficult virtue to learn and maintain. As a society we reward arrogance and "attitude"; and our heroes tend to be loud and brash sports figures, millionaire developers, movie stars, and the like—those kinds of people who don't know, or don't want to know, what humility is. But of all the virtues, humility is the one that life will teach us if we don't learn it of our own accord.

Two young men were hunting far from their village one day

long ago during a time of great hardship for their people. A great drought had driven the animals from their usual territories, but the people themselves seemed to have lost their way as well. They were weak and unhappy, yielding to confusion and anger because they had forgotten the good ways that had made them strong.

The young hunters had not been successful and were discouraged, but they kept to the trail nonetheless. One morning they saw a strange sight at the top of a hill, a floating white mist. They had not seen clouds for many months and were curious, but also afraid. With much caution they approached the floating mist.

From out of the mist came a woman, a very beautiful young woman, and she was naked. The hunters were astonished, of course, and didn't know what to do. One of them immediately had impure thoughts and approached the young woman, intending to take full advantage of the situation. The second hunter tried to stop him, to no avail. Before the first hunter could reach the young woman the mist rolled down and covered him and in a while it rolled back. The other hunter was terrified to see that his companion was now nothing more than a skeleton. His flesh had been consumed by the mist and snakes were crawling in and around the bones.

Realizing that he was in the presence of something mysterious and powerful, the remaining hunter humbled himself before the young woman. She spoke, commending him for his humility and gave him a task. He was to return immediately to his village with instructions for his people to prepare a lodge for her. Then they were to wait for her to come.

The young hunter did as he was told, convincing the people of his village that they should do as the young woman had asked. Soon after the lodge was prepared the young woman appeared with a bundle in her arms. Inviting the elders into the lodge she taught them seven ceremonies they must perform faithfully. If they did as she instructed, they would once again become powerful and flourish. Opening her bundle she revealed to them a sacred pipe. She taught them how to use the pipe, and then she departed.

The people watched as she walked to the top of a hill where a floating white mist had appeared. The young woman walked into the mist and emerged from the other side as a female white buffalo.

This is, of course, a condensed version of the most revered of Lakota stories: the coming of the White Buffalo Calf Maiden. She brought us not only the pipe, which we still have to this day, but also the basis for our spiritual beliefs and the ceremonies through which we carry them out. But there are two simple lessons in this story that are often overlooked.

We did as the White Buffalo Calf Maiden instructed us to do. We followed the ceremonies and lived in the good ways she taught us, and we became strong. In fact, we became the most powerful people on the Plains, although I shudder to think what might have happened if both hunters had been brash and arrogant.

But I think the White Buffalo Calf Maiden appeared to these two particular young men precisely because one was arrogant and one was humble. The first lesson is that arrogance was destroyed. The White Buffalo Calf Maiden had no use for it, and the mist that covered the arrogant hunter is life itself. The second lesson is that humility was used as an instrument for good.

Most of us have been at times generous, brave, respectful, and even wise. But humility is the one virtue that validates all the others. The people in No Moccasins' village honored her for her humility rather than for the courageous deed she performed as a young woman. Likewise, though Crazy Horse was the bravest of the brave on the battlefield and his exploits are legendary, those who knew him best spoke more often of the humble, quiet way he lived life. But the fact is there are also the

Iktomis of the world: those who hide behind the illusion of arrogance and can make it seem real and appealing.

A humble person rarely stumbles, the old ones say, because such a person walks with face toward the Earth and can see the path ahead. On the other hand, the arrogant man who walks with his head high to bask in the glory of the moment will stumble often because he is more concerned with the moment than what lays ahead.

The Lakota warriors of old who took part in the *waktoglaka* and publicly recounted their deeds had every right to feel proud of their accomplishments and accept the honor they had earned. They understood, and were often reminded, that it was the deed or deeds performed under the most difficult of circumstances that earned them honor, not the telling. And if the honor for a deed well done was accepted with humility, it only served to increase the worth of the honor and enhanced a man's reputation.

The burden of humility is light because a truly humble person divests himself or herself of the need for recognition. The burden of arrogance, on the other hand, grows heavier day by day. In sharing the journey of life, travel with the humble person on the quiet path.

2

Perseverance

Wowacintanka (wo-wah-chin-tan-gah)

To persist, to strive in spite of difficulties

✠ The Story of the Giants

There's a long ridge north of Highway 16 in central Tripp
County, South Dakota, in the prairie country west of the Missouri River (once called the Great Muddy). It looks out of place,
that ridge, not exactly fitting in with the flatlands around it. It
looks to me like someone put it there after the prairies were
made. I've heard there was a time when that ridge was not there.

They say it was a summer of many storms that time when Red
Calf's people were camped on the prairie north of the Running
Water River and south of the Great Muddy. Cloud and Plum
were married in the Moon of Berries Ripening—May. Two
evenings later a storm blew in from the southwest, so fierce that
the old ones said it was the worst one they ever knew. The
winged ones stayed out of the sky, two-leggeds stayed inside
shelter, and four-leggeds hid inside thickets. Women braved
cold raindrops and stinging hailstones to pound in picket pins
so the buffalo hide lodges would stand strong in the howling
winds. The night sentinels covered their heads with buffalo
robes as they stood watch. Big black clouds rolled across the sky

and the Thunders shouted, their mighty voices crackling and rumbling, and their angry eyes flashing with the light of a hundred suns.

But that storm was not the worst thing that happened to Red Calf's people that summer. While they waited out the wind, rain, and hailstones, something dark and ugly came out of the night, ripping into their lodges.

Cloud and Plum huddled together in their new home pitched behind her parents' lodge as the great storm rumbled and blew. Their lodge stood strong in the wind, however, and they knew it would pass as all storms do. But from the darkness they heard cries of fear, of terror. Dogs barked and howled in fright; men shouted warnings that were lost in the wind. Women and children screamed.

Something ripped their lodge from its picket pins, something more powerful than the wind. A mountainous black figure, far taller than the lodge, stood outlined against the lightening flashes. It was *Iya,* the Giant, with the strength of a thousand men, the blackest of hearts, and a bottomless hunger that drove him to terrible deeds.

A hand larger than a grown man reached in and snatched Plum away from Cloud, like someone plucking a new leaf. Before Cloud's unbelieving eyes the hand tossed the struggling Plum into a mouth like a large hole in the ground, and she was gone. He was shocked and couldn't move as Iya tore apart the village to satisfy his ravenous hunger.

Many lodges were torn apart that night, many minds were numb with fear as Iya swept through the village; no one nor anything could stop him. Cloud and a few other young men pulled themselves together to grab bows and send arrows at the giant, but the thing paid them no heed. Iya grabbed girls and young women and tossed them into his wide, slobbering mouth. Then he was gone into the blackness of the stormy night, leaving behind torn, scattered lodges, confusion, and grieving hearts.

By dawn the storm weakened and the people began to put their village back together, but they could only grieve for their precious ones snatched up by the giant. Red Calf gathered the council of old men together to consider what to do.

It is no use to do anything, some said. Iya was too big and powerful. The only thing to do is to move the village and hope he doesn't return, some advised.

Women began to take down the lodges in preparation for the move and men gathered the travois dogs to pull the loads, for this happened in the time before horses came. Cloud didn't intend to make the move. He was angry. Iya had taken his new wife, and he could only imagine her pain and terror. He went to his mother and father and announced that he would gather his weapons and strike out after Iya.

Word spread quickly of Cloud's plan and seven others joined him. Soon eight stalwart young men headed east armed with lances, knives, and bows and arrows—and a terrible anger. Iya's trail was easy to follow. His footprints were so deep that rainwater gathered in them.

Red Calf led the people north toward the Great Muddy River as the eight young men took the trail of revenge after Iya. After half a day's travel they found him asleep on a hillside, far enough away to look small. When they were a long bow shot from him Iya awoke. They hid and watched as the giant stretched and scratched. He was an ugly beast, naked and unwashed with twigs and branches caught in his long tangled hair. He scowled with the air of someone with nothing to fear.

Cloud and the others had never seen Iya. They knew him as an imaginary creature in the stories told by the old ones, a fiction made up to scare them into behaving. Grandma Little Bird would only smile secretively when he or his sister Shawl, as small children, would ask if Iya was real. Now there he sat, bigger than any living thing Cloud had ever seen. And somewhere inside his stomach were Plum and all the other girls and young women the thing had snatched up.

Cloud had never felt so small. He was a fine hunter, helping his father to keep his family fed and clothed since he was twelve winters old. He already had a good reputation as a fighting man, a warrior. But on the hunt or the warpath he had never faced anything like Iya. His cousin Black Fox asked the question on all their minds.

"How will we defeat such a thing?"

No one could answer.

"We will think of something," was all Cloud could say.

Iya arose and walked eastward, flattening everything in his path. Rabbits, deer, and antelope scurried out of his way and the birds in the air flew away from him.

They followed him the day long until the giant stopped at dusk to sleep in a gully. They could hear him snoring. The young men made camp without fires so as not to attract Iya's attention. They rested and ate *wasna* (pemmican), and talked in whispers, not knowing how sharp his ears were. Cloud suddenly thought of a way to kill him.

"We will trap him," he announced.

"How can we trap him?" fretted Slow, who worried about everything. "He is stronger than all the men in the village put together."

"True," agreed Cloud, "but he has a weakness. In the stories he was always hungry. Remember? That is his weakness; we will use it to trap him. We will offer him food."

"You are crazy!" retorted Slow, "we are his food! Will you offer one of us?"

"Yes," replied Cloud patiently. "I will offer myself; I will get him to chase me and then I will lead him to the trap."

"What trap?"

"A hole. A hole in the ground that we will dig."

"You *are* crazy!" said Yellow Hawk. "How can we dig a hole big enough for Iya?"

"Do you care for your sister enough to try?" asked Cloud. "Do you want to end her suffering and take her home? Me, I want my wife back. I will do what I must because I do not want to live without her!"

Through the night they talked about Cloud's idea. Six would dig a hole while two of them—Cloud and one other—would decoy Iya and lead him to the trap. When the new day dawned they went forth with determination.

The place they chose for the trap was a dried up creek in a flat plain where the ground was sandy and easy to dig. They quickly made stone axes. Two deer were killed for meat to feed the diggers because they would work night and day. When the digging started, Cloud and Yellow Hawk left to find the giant. They would need to keep him decoyed until the signal was given that the trap was ready. Then they would lead him to it.

They thought Iya was dimwitted and counted on that to help them, but something else turned out to be more helpful. They found him easily when they went downwind of him. Iya smelled bad because he never bathed and could be located at great distances when the wind was right.

Slow and the others dug and dug. The thought of their loved ones suffering inside Iya's stomach gave them strength. Dirt piled up on both sides of the trench as they dug deeper and deeper.

Iya slept for most of two days. After awakening he wandered aimlessly across the prairies. Everywhere he went the animals and birds fled from his path.

Days and nights passed. The diggers worked without rest. Out on the prairie Iya suddenly set out with long strides. Cloud and Yellow Hawk ran to keep pace. They had to do something to stop him.

After sunset they built a fire to attract his attention. When he came to it they built another about an arrow's cast away. Using that simple trick they were able to lead him back to the west. Each time he came to one fire they stole away into the darkness to build another. In the daylight they made heavy smoke by piling green grass on the fires to attract his attention.

All went well for a time until Iya spotted them. Dimwitted though he was, he did have keen eyesight. With a roar of surprise and anger he stumbled after them.

The ground shook. Iya's feet were like boulders crashing to the earth. One of his strides was twenty of theirs, yet they were able to stay away from him, sometimes going in opposite directions to confuse him. It was a dangerous game that went on and on, and Cloud and Yellow Hawk grew tired because they could not rest or eat. They shouted encouragement back and forth, reminding one another that they must save their women.

Back on the prairie the trench was growing deeper. Slow and the others worked their fingers and knuckles bloody. They broke several stone axes and made new ones. They used knives and lance points, too. Of course they had no way of knowing how it was with Cloud and Yellow Hawk or if the ugly giant could be lured to the trap, but they kept digging even as several sunrises and sunsets rolled by. No one slept because the thought of their women inside the ugly giant's stomach was enough to make them dig harder and harder.

Slow measured the depth of the trench and found it to be as deep as five men standing on top of one another. It was finished. Now it was time to signal to Cloud and Yellow Hawk.

They gathered driftwood from a nearby creek and dried brush from a grove to cover the trench. Then a large pile of dried wood was arranged atop one ridge of dirt and set ablaze, the signal for Cloud and Yellow Hawk.

Iya was sleeping again, which was good because Cloud and Yellow Hawk needed to rest and eat. They suddenly saw a fire in the distance and knew what it meant. Slow, Black Fox, and the others had finished the trap!

Yellow Hawk's leg was still hurting. Iya had nearly grabbed him but he had been able to slip from his grasp. He had tumbled down into a gully and badly wrenched his knee.

Cloud hid Yellow Hawk in a low plum thicket. Iya had nearly

stepped on them several times as he searched for them, yelling his frustration.

Now the trap was ready and Iya had to be lured to it. Cloud would be the bait by himself. Yellow Hawk was angry because he couldn't help and Cloud had to convince him to stay hidden.

Cloud prepared himself. He prayed and made offerings. Making sure Yellow Hawk was well hidden, he went after the angry and dangerous Iya.

It was easy to find Iya and easier to get him to follow. To him Cloud was a little pest to be crushed. With a roar like thunder he took up the chase. To stay alive Cloud had to keep out of the giant's long reach.

The chase continued through the day. Cloud was tiring, but the thought of Plum inside the giant gave him courage. From the top of a rise he could see the enormous piles of earth thrown up by Slow and the others. Iya was growing tired also, but he kept going because he was hungry. Cloud led him across the prairie and toward the mouth of the trench.

Slow and his companions saw Iya approaching and hid. If the ruse worked and Iya fell into the trench, they had to loosen the abutments that would collapse the mounds of earth into the trench. Closer and closer Iya came, looming larger and larger. Then they saw a figure running before him. It was Cloud and it was plain that he was near the end of his endurance, stumbling badly and falling every few steps.

Cloud had thrown away his weapons since they were useless against Iya. Soaked in sweat he ran only on sheer will power. He fell many times and each time fought mightily to regain his feet and push on. If he didn't, the giant would crush him like an insect with one swat.

Down a grassy slope Cloud lost his footing and slid to the bottom. Iya's hand came down like a falling tree. Cloud rolled aside to barely avoid being flattened. He had no more strength in his arms and legs and his mind was numb—he was too exhausted to be afraid. He had given everything he had, and could do no more. Closing his eyes he waited for Iya to crush the life out of him. Then he saw Plum in her wedding dress, the soft smile on her beautiful face, her dark eyes full of hope and love. He saw two small children, a boy and a girl playing along the banks of the Smoking Earth River. Cloud knew that the images he saw were his dreams. Dreams inspired by Plum.

Somewhere deep within he found a pebble of strength, one last spark of hope to save Plum, to make their dreams come true. With a bellow of rage, like a newborn's cry of life, he rolled away from Iya's outstretched fingers and leaped to his feet.

The ground shook as Iya lurched forward. Cloud somehow made his legs move and led Iya toward the covered hole he knew was there. Slow and the others watched, barely breathing, as the giant, kicking up clods of dirt, lumbered toward their hiding places. Cloud saw the brush over the opening and knew he had to carefully place his feet. Behind him Iya's mouth, nearly as wide as a lodge, was curled into a snarl, his yellow teeth bared and his long, black hair swirling about like black smoke.

Cloud was halfway across the covered trench when he heard Slow's shout of triumph quickly drowned out by Iya's cry of surprise and a loud cracking. He flung himself off the brush covering barely a heartbeat before it gave way. Iya was far too heavy for the brush covering. He broke through it and down into the trench.

Iya fell to the bottom with a great thud and was caught firmly in the hole. Dust billowed upward as he struggled, filling the air with his deafening yells of rage.

Slow dragged Cloud to safety and signaled Black Fox to collapse the abutments holding the dirt piles. The dirt slid down into the trench. A huge cloud of dust rose upward. Iya's roars turned to frightened whimpers. His free arm reached up and one hand clawed at the edge of the hole. His legs were caught firmly and he could not free himself.

He struggled with all his might, coughing as dirt covered his massive head. Soon his struggles weakened, and he coughed no more. His leg twitched a last time and a silence fell over the land.

A limping Yellow Hawk appeared and all the young men stood gaping at the dead giant. Somehow they had defeated it, but there was no joy, no feeling of victory. Grabbing a knife Cloud jumped down into the trench and began to slice open Iya's stomach. By no means was it a pleasant task. Foul air and a greenish-yellow slime leaked out.

Cloud yelled for help as he reached in and pulled out the body of a girl covered in slime, more dead than alive. But she was alive! There was hope for the others. With a yell of triumph the seven other young men jumped down into the pit as Cloud enlarged the opening and found more bodies.

All the young women and girls were still alive, but barely. The young men pulled them out of the giant's stomach and hauled them out of the trench and then quickly to the nearby stream. In its cool waters they were gently revived and cleaned.

Plum regained her senses and felt her husband's gentle hands washing her face, and wept for joy. There were many tears of joy that day.

The young men filled in the hole to cover Iya's body, and the dirt piled higher and higher until it became a long ridge. In time grass and cactus grew on it.

Cloud and Plum grew old together. They raised two children along the way—a boy and a girl—and treasured the laughter of several grandchildren. Cloud wore the blue blanket of headman for many winters, after accepting it from old Red Calf. The people followed him because they knew him to be wise as well as brave.

On stormy summer nights Plum would gather her grandchildren and tell them the story of a terrible, ugly giant. The little ones would ask Grandma Plum if giants were real, and she would only smile—secretively. So would Grandpa Cloud.

It was so long ago, that Summer of Many Storms, in the days before the coming of horses. Plum, Cloud, Yellow Hawk, Black

Fox, and all the others live only in stories now. The same is true of Iya. But there is a long ridge covered with grass and cactus, running east to west.

Many people drive by it every day. To most it is only a long hill. A few of us, though, still remember the story of how Iya was defeated. We know that ridge is his grave. But in our hearts we think of it more as something built by love, courage, and perseverance, and by giants.

The Meaning of Eight Miles

Working for the Civilian Conservation Corps (CCC) in the 1930s, my grandfather Albert Two Hawk, then nearly fifty years old, was part of a construction crew building a dam. To get to work he arose at four o'clock in the morning, walked eight miles to the job site, and then walked all day guiding (more like wrestling) a four-foot-wide dirt scoop pulled by a team of four horses. When the day's work was done, he unharnessed his horses; fed, watered, and put them in their pen; and walked eight miles home. This was his routine six days a week for several months. When I was about five and he was sixty-two, I watched him build a log house mostly on his own, with only hand tools. That was the first time I recall thinking my grandfather could do anything. Looking back on it now, anyone who can build a house while a five-year-old boy is underfoot in every conceivable manner is capable of miracles.

My grandfather was a man of many talents. He could wield an ax, a bucksaw, a hammer, or a butcher knife with consummate skill. He could skin and quarter a deer or a steer faster than anyone, and make skillet bread over a campfire. In such ways he was like many Lakota men of his generation, but there was something that set him apart. My grandfather had something that isn't dependent on a skill or strength. He knew how to persevere.

My grandfather certainly had the requisite skills to do the job for the CCC. He knew horses, for example, and wasn't afraid of hard work. The dollar or so he earned every day during the Depression went a long way to support his family—my grandmother, my mother, my uncle. But walking eight miles to work, in addition to many, many miles on the job, and then eight miles home—only to do it again the following day—required more than ability or physical strength.

I can't imagine the bone-weary fatigue he must have felt each night. My grandmother said he would arrive home, eat, and fall into bed. It's one thing to succumb to fatigue at the end of an exhausting day; it is quite another thing to wake up before dawn and persuade yourself to do it all over again. That is where perseverance kicks in.

Perseverance rises from the spirit—rather like a sleeping giant—when we've reached our physical limits or we've collided with a barrier that tells us we can't or shouldn't. It enhances strengths and capabilities, awakens our determination, and enables us to move beyond our limits, coaxing from us just enough effort to keep moving, to keep reaching and striving despite the weariness, or pain, or despair.

There were moments, I'm sure, when my grandfather felt as if he were battling with a giant that summer working for the CCC. He was at that time still in his physical prime and he was a very strong man. But it was more than physical strength that kept him going.

There was, of course, adequate motivation to push himself day in and day out. He had a family. But for every story of a man (or woman) who makes sacrifices for family, we hear of one or more who abandons family, who leaves and is never seen again. What makes the difference? What does the man or woman who makes sacrifices have that the one who leaves doesn't? Love of family, selflessness, a sense of commitment? It's safe to say that both the one who makes sacrifices and the one who leaves had examples to follow. Chances are that the man or woman who makes sacrifices had someone in his or her life who exemplified commitment, or perseverance. Perhaps he or she heard a story about defeating a giant.

The truth is, anyone can persevere. And why is perseverance a necessary virtue? Because sometimes, perhaps too many times, it is the only answer, the only course of action left. My grandfather had to persevere in order that his family could make it through some extremely difficult times. Where did he find his example? In a sense, my grandfather had examples of perseverance all around him. His people had to survive individually and as a group by using the last weapon in their arsenal—perseverance.

The only person who could have led an effective, organized military resistance against the whites was the Oglala Lakota leader Crazy Horse. Crazy Horse was killed at Fort Robinson, Nebraska, in September of 1877 as a result of the jealousy of some Lakota and the gross misunderstanding and paranoia of white military commanders. The old ways were gone, the wars to repel the whites were over, and rising to prominence in Lakota political circles depended on currying favor with the whites. Crazy Horse was the last Oglala to have the unquestioning loyalty of his people that was so desired by many other would-be leaders, and there was jealousy. The white commanders were afraid of his influence over the many Lakota fighting men who would readily follow him against them. Thus the few jealous Lakota fomented a rumor that Crazy Horse was planning to kill the commanding general. The commanding general took the bait and attempted to have Crazy Horse incarcerated. As he physically resisted the attempt to jail him, a soldier stabbed him with a bayonet.

The only other leader at the time who could have rallied enough fighting men to him to be a serious threat was the Hunkpapa Lakota Sitting Bull. But the U.S. Army had stepped up its campaign against the Lakota as a result of the defeat of the Seventh Cavalry at Little Bighorn in 1876. So in 1877,

Sitting Bull was in Canada seeking sanctuary from the pursuit of the government. There was, therefore, no way for the Lakota to resist militarily. Sitting Bull was killed in 1890 primarily because of the same kind of paranoia the government displayed in the situation regarding Crazy Horse. In 1889 and 1890 the Lakota embraced the Ghost Dance movement—begun in the Southwest by a Paiute Indian—which advocated performing a special dance that would put them in touch with dead ancestors and help bring back the old life before the coming of whites. The government saw this as nothing more than the basis for a military uprising, one that could be given impetus if Sitting Bull were to join. To prevent that, they attempted to arrest him, and during that attempt Sitting Bull was shot and killed. With him, then, died the last possibility of a strong, organized resistance to white encroachment. Therefore, when resistance ceased to be an option, surviving within the parameters of white control on the reservations was the only choice. There was no other option but to reach deep inside and persevere day in and day out, year in and year out, from one generation to the next.

Persevering in these circumstances meant ensuring that our language, our traditions, customs, values—the essence of what we are as Lakota—survived as long as possible. The first generation of Lakota to cope with life on the reservation could no longer defend themselves on the field of battle, so they fought with the only weapon at their disposal: spiritual strength. That spiritual strength, that willingness to persevere in the face of forced change has enabled my generation to stand not only on our own as Lakota, but also on the shoulders of those who went before—those who faced the giant and showed us how to persevere.

I asked my grandfather, after finally gathering up the nerve to ask him about his dam-building experience, how he had faced the giant. He said he had no other choice at the time, and then he told me a story about a lazy man.

There was a young man, he said, who had a hard time doing

anything for himself, so out of concern his family waited on him hand and foot. But that only made matters worse. After a time the young man couldn't, or wouldn't, get out of his own bed. Eventually he wouldn't take the trouble to lift a spoon to his mouth when meals were brought to him, so a sister had to feed him. The years passed and the young man became an adult who was like a helpless infant. He had to be bathed and dressed and, of course, hand fed every day. As his parents grew older it was difficult for them to care for him, and his younger sister passed up offers of marriage in order to care for her lazy brother. For that's all he was, simply lazy. In time the lazy man's parents died, and he finally decided that the best thing he could do for his sister was to be taken to his grave to wait to die himself. The entire village agreed that it was the only honorable thing for him to do, so his sister tearfully agreed. On the appointed day, as he was being carried to his grave, a distraught relative stopped his pall-bearers, offering a gift of armloads of corn in an effort to stop the man from killing himself. The lazy man asked if the corn was husked. The answer was no. "Then," the lazy man said to his pallbearers, "keep going."

My grandfather was, of course, modestly saying that he didn't want to be thought of as a lazy man. But he was also saying that if one doesn't find a way to do what is necessary, it's easier the next time to find a way not to act. Furthermore, if one can do the necessary and sometimes seemingly mundane things, one has it within himself or herself to persevere when it becomes necessary.

In the 1964 Tokyo Olympics, Billy Mills, the Oglala Lakota (Pine Ridge Sioux) long-distance runner competing for the United States, found a way to persevere when no one, especially his coaches, thought he could keep up with the other runners—much less win. He won the Gold Medal in the grueling ten-thousand-meter race.

Lloyd Moses, a Sicangu Lakota (Rosebud Sioux), rose to the rank of major general in the United States Army in the 1960s, the first of his tribe to do so and one of a few Native Americans to achieve flag rank in any branch of the United States military. Dr. Ben Reifel, another Rosebud Sioux, was elected to and served several terms in the U.S. House of Representatives in the late 1950s and early 1960s. After that stint he served as a consultant to the National Park Service.

Billy Mills had several reasons to reach down deep inside and find a way to persevere. The most immediate were his competitors, the other runners. But the most compelling reason was the attitude of the coaches who didn't think that Mills was in the same class as his competitors. Lieutenant Mills (he was in the United States Marine Corps at the time) won his race and proved a point. There is virtually nothing that can defeat perseverance—not fatigue, not pain, and not prejudice.

Major General Lloyd Moses and Dr. Ben Reifel achieved military rank and political stature at a time when many white Americans assumed that Native Americans couldn't succeed in American society. How and why did they succeed? Ability and hard work certainly had much to do with their achievements, as is the case with anyone who succeeds. But because of what they were, Lloyd Moses, Ben Reifel, and Billy Mills had an added obstacle: the expectation that they would eventually fail. Of course, when someone is expected to fail, there is little encouragement. And when encouragement from others is largely absent, people like Moses, Reifel, and Mills find it where it is most readily available: from within. That is the first step to perseverance.

My grandmother Annie Nellie Two Hawk was a widow for nine years. I gained a new perspective about her during those years, perhaps because it was strange to see her without my grandfather. Unnatural would be more like it, because they had been married for fifty-five years when he died in 1975. And in my world one had never been without the other. My grandmother without my grandfather was sunrise without sunset, thunder without lightening. Though I'd always been close to her (she and Grandpa Albert raised me), I learned a lot about, and from, Grandma Nellie over those years she was a widow mainly because she shared or retold stories about herself before she married my grandfather. She wept keenly when she described the loss of her younger sister Fannie to Spanish influenza in 1919. Grandma Nellie was then nineteen and Fannie was eighteen. The most important lesson for me was the realization that she lived those nine years the same way she did the previous seventy-five: with dignity, calmness of spirit, selflessness, and perseverance. She found a way to reach deep inside to everything she was and had seen to deal with the profound loneliness she felt without my grandfather.

There have been moments in my life when Iya has come out of the darkness to overwhelm me and make me feel insignificant and not equal to the task, whether it was recovering from a broken hip or surviving the passing of my precious grandparents. Sometimes the giant has been so large and menacing that I have forgotten that within me is the means to defeat him. Within me, as within everyone, is the ability to persevere. Then I remind myself that darkness, despair, pain, and the absence of hope are what perseverance thrives on. When friends and colleagues seem to have deserted because you have made and stuck by an unpopular decision; when the specter of racial or gender bias has slammed a seemingly immovable obstacle in your path; when the weight of loneliness appears to have made you invisible to the world; when going to a job you don't like makes you hate going through the front door; when facing a teacher whose only purpose is to make you so miserable even tying your shoe laces seems an impossible task; or when failure shakes your self-confidence, that's the time to pause and reach inside—and try again.

You can't truly succeed without perseverance. If you've easily accomplished many goals, you are indeed fortunate. But as my grandfather would often say, life isn't worth living unless you are forced to defend it now and then. Therefore you haven't truly tasted success unless you've picked yourself up after failure has knocked you down, as many times as it takes, until you accomplish what you've set out to do.

If I have within me one-tenth of my grandparents' ability to meet adversity, I can face anything. I'm reminded of that each time I see a stock dam anywhere, because it reminds me of one such dam called the Blue Rock Dam near White River, South Dakota, in what was the northern part of the Rosebud Reservation. The Blue Rock Dam is eight miles from where my parents now live, on the home site on which Grandpa Albert and Grandma Nellie once lived. Eight miles is a long walk, but each step is a lesson in perseverance.

3

Respect

Wawoohola (wah-wo-o-ho-lah)

To be considerate, to hold in high esteem

The Story of the Deer Woman

I have never seen the Deer Woman myself, but I heard of a man who did when I was a boy. My grandmother knew that man—a young man, she said. He was always restless; he was never home. He didn't pay attention to his young wife, she said, because he couldn't stop looking for the Deer Woman. That could happen to me, she warned, if I wasn't careful.

No one I know these days has seen the Deer Woman. Maybe it's because we Lakota are too modern and what we used to believe has been watered down, you might say. Maybe the Deer Woman knows we wouldn't respect what she is if she did show herself to someone in these times. Still, every time I went hunting I thought I might see her. There was still some lonely country when I was a young man, before farms and ranches took over: quiet river valleys thick with oak and cottonwood, and wide-open prairies where nothing moved but the wind—the kind of places I heard the Deer Woman liked to show herself to a lone hunter.

It's one thing to think ahead about what to do, but when

something does happen, it's never the way you imagined it would be. So I don't know what I would have done if the Deer Woman had appeared to me. I like to think I would have done the right thing, that is, not given in to her, as in the story my grandmother used to tell me of a young man in the old, old days. I've forgotten the young man's name so we'll just call him *Koskalaka (ko-shkah-lah-kah),* which means "young man" in Lakota.

When he was a boy Koskalaka lived with his grandmother. His grandfather had died so the boy's mother and father decided he should live with his grandmother. He didn't go all that far because her lodge was next to theirs.

The boy helped his grandmother by doing chores, but mainly he kept her from being lonely. In return she told him stories and taught him to cook, make clothes, and so on. The stories were what he liked best—stories of how the people came into the world through a hole in the ground; of the White Buffalo Calf Maiden, who brought the pipe to the people and taught them many good things; and of the strong warriors in his family. There were so many stories he wondered if he could remember them all.

One evening in the middle of a long winter, when the snow outside was deep and the winds howled, the old woman told her grandson the story of the Deer Woman.

"Grandson," she began, "I have something to tell you." That's how some old people began their stories. "You are learning to be a hunter, and to be a hunter is a good thing. A good hunter provides for his family so that there can be food to eat and good clothing to wear. I know you will be a fine hunter, and I also know you will hunt alone many times. When you are alone hunting there is something you must watch out for, something besides the animals like the bear and the great cat who can hurt you, something besides the enemies who come into our country now and then.

"Sometimes the danger waiting out there is not just that your body might be injured or wounded. Sometimes the danger is for your spirit, too.

"Men are sometimes wounded in battle or they are hurt while hunting. Those wounds or injuries can heal, but your spirit is a different thing. If your spirit is hurt, sometimes it can never be well.

"My husband, your grandfather, told me of something that I heard of when I was a little girl—something out there always waiting for hunters. He saw her, he told me, when he was a young man, before he became my husband. Maybe you will see her, too.

"The Deer Woman waits out there, Grandson. When you are a young man and a hunter and you go out alone, she might appear to you. When you are tired and hungry and very far from home, perhaps when your hunt has not been good, she will come to you.

"She is the most beautiful woman any man has seen. Those that have seen her say so. Her hair is shiny and hangs to her ankles, her eyes are large and sparkle with a light that beckons, and her smile can turn the strongest man into a foolish boy.

"Her lodge is always pitched nearby, with a fire inside, and soft robes. She will invite you in to drink tea with her, to rest.

"Do not go near her, Grandson. Do not go near her lodge. Some men have and their spirits were taken by her. They went into her lodge with her, and they rested; they lay with her as if she were wife to them. When they woke up, they found themselves alone. The lodge was gone; she was gone. They had known her; they had lain with her, the most beautiful woman they had ever seen. And she was all they could think of.

"When this happens to a man, young or old, he forgets his family and goes looking for her, the Deer Woman. But he can never find her, no matter where he looks; no matter how far he travels, he can never find her. Such a man goes looking for the

Deer Woman, he tells himself, because she is so beautiful that he must have her. But he is really looking for his spirit because she has taken it from him. A man who has lain with her is never the same; he is always restless.

"So when you are a young man, Grandson, and you are hunting alone far from home and you come across the most beautiful woman you have ever seen, you must turn away. If you go with her, she will please you and she will give you pleasure; but she will also take your spirit from you and you will never have it back. It may be the most difficult thing you will ever do, but you must turn away from her."

Koskalaka did grow up to be a fine hunter. He was the best hunter in the village, as a matter of fact. He never failed to provide for his family and for those who were needy. It was said of him that when he left the village on the hunt, two things would be for certain: He would not return empty-handed and he would be gone for many days.

One autumn, soon after his grandmother had died, Koskalaka made preparations for a hunt. He told his mother and father he would travel with three other hunters and they would be gone longer than usual because it had been a dry summer and the animals were closer to the big river, far to the north.

The hunters reached the big river and set up their camp. They hunted the deep gullies and draws that cut down to the river's banks. They were successful, but they had to use every skill they knew because the deer and elk were not so plentiful as they usually were, and, they seemed especially wary. Because the hunters were so far from home, they also had to dry the meat they had killed. As the days wore on they grew tired and were anxious to go home.

Just before sundown one evening, Koskalaka tracked a bull elk to learn the trail the animal used each day. He was certain he could bring it down the next day if he waited in ambush at a good spot. As he headed back for the hunting camp, he smelled smoke from a fire and decided to see if enemies were about. Sneaking carefully down into a wide gully, he found a lone *tipi*, a lodge, pitched in a grove of oak. It was a fine lodge, but a small one, and Koskalaka wondered if others had come to the big river valleys to hunt.

As he watched the lodge to see who might return to it, a woman came out and looked in his direction. He waited, but he could see no one else. The woman waved and walked toward the plum thicket he was hiding in until she was very close.

"You must be very tired." Her voice was soft and soothing. Koskalaka stepped from the thicket and a shudder went up his back. Standing before him was the most beautiful woman he had ever seen in his life. There were several beautiful woman back in his small village, but their beauty next to this one was like the dim glow of a campfire next to the brightness of the moon.

"I have a fire; it is warm in my lodge and there are robes to rest on. Come," she said, her eyes beckoning and filled with promises a young man could not mistake.

Koskalaka knew who she was, of course. Standing a few steps from him was the Deer Woman. All the stories he had heard were true. She was so beautiful that he couldn't take his eyes from her. Her hair was black as night and hung to her slender ankles. Her hands were small and delicate. Her eyes were deep, deep brown and very large with thick, long lashes. A man could get lost in them. A soft smile curved her full lips upward. And there was the slight scent of rose hips as if her finely tanned dress had been rubbed with the flowers.

"I know you are tired," she went on, smiling. "Come into my lodge and rest."

Koskalaka trembled. There was something more to this creature before him, he could feel it. He was afraid, but he was also tempted. He wanted to follow her, to take her into her lodge.

She turned and walked away for a few steps, her slender body swaying, her long hair swinging with the fringe of her dress. She stopped and turned to Koskalaka. "You are strong, a fine young man," she murmured. "I am looking for a young man such as you. I have been waiting for you. Come."

Koskalaka's legs seemed to have a mind of their own. Before he knew what was happening he was walking toward the Deer Woman, his hand reaching for her outstretched hand. But a heartbeat before his hand touched hers he stopped.

"No!" he said, pulling his hand back. "I will not go with you."

"Yes, you must," she replied, her voice soft and low, her eyes leaving no doubt as to her meaning. "I need you."

Koskalaka was a strong young man, strong of body and of mind. It took all of that strength to turn away from the Deer Woman. It was the voice in his head that helped him—a voice that said, "It may be the most difficult thing you will ever do, but you must turn away from her."

"No," Koskalaka said again, "I will not go with you. My grandmother said that I must turn away from you. I will not go with you; leave me alone."

Deer Woman's beautiful face quickly twisted into an angry sneer. She stamped her feet and snorted. Her mouth moved, but she could not speak.

A cold wind suddenly sprang up, scattering the leaves in the gully. Koskalaka was afraid and he turned to run. Leaves rattled all around him and he heard a whistling snort, the sound deer made when they were alarmed. Looking back he saw a deer standing where the Deer Woman had been. It was a female blacktail with a dark stripe across its face. He had never seen such a black stripe across the face of any deer. Koskalaka noticed something else. The Deer Woman's lodge was gone.

The deer lowered its head to charge. Koskalaka put an arrow on his bow string and raised his bow to take aim. The deer spun and disappeared into a line of sumac. Never again in his life would Koskalaka see such a deer, although he would always be on the lookout for it, for her. He never saw the Deer Woman again for as long as he lived.

Koskalaka returned to the hunting camp and told his companions what had happened. He told them he had seen the Deer Woman. They believed him because there was something different about him; there was a look of strength in his eyes.

"We must build a sweat lodge and pray," he told them. So they did—a low round lodge made of willow and covered with deer and elk hides. That night they heated stones and made a sweat to purify themselves and to pray for good things to happen.

In the days that followed their hunting was good; it was very good. Soon they had plenty of meat to take home.

In time Koskalaka courted a young woman from another village and won her love. They married and had a son and a daughter. Over the years not only was he the finest, most skillful hunter to come along in many a generation, but he was also a stalwart warrior and a leader of men. Men were willing to follow him on the warpath or on the hunt because he had a calm manner and strength of spirit. And when he was an older man, he took his place on the council of old men, and there he was known for his wisdom and good advice.

The Deer Woman couldn't fool Koskalaka because of one thing: respect. Koskalaka loved and respected his grandmother. And because he did, he remembered her words during that awful moment when the Deer Woman almost took him. If he hadn't respected his grandmother, he would not have remembered what she had told him.

Perhaps the Deer Woman doesn't appear to lone hunters anymore. Or perhaps she does in other ways. Times have changed for us, so maybe she's changed her ways, too, and comes after our spirits in other ways. I can tell you one thing: You're never too old to remember the things your grandmother taught you. It's never too late to respect the ways of our elders. It's never too late to remember what Grandmother said.

Remembering Respect

Luther Standing Bear, a Lakota and one of the first Native American writers to be published (around 1900), talked about respect as an essential ingredient for balanced interaction among all living things. According to him, the Lakota had developed a respect for the Earth and all forms of life because all were a necessary part of the physical environment. He suggested that some people, and he was politely implicating whites, had lost respect for animals. His biggest concern was that humans who lost respect for animals would soon lose respect for their own kind as well. Unfortunately, human history is replete with horrifying examples of mindless cruelty that bear out Standing Bear's fears: the Spanish Inquisition, the African slave trade, the Salem witch trials, the black hole of Calcutta, the Wounded Knee massacre of 1890, the Bataan death march, the Holocaust, the My Lai massacre of 1968, and so on. I suppose it could be argued that there were many other contributing factors in each of those events, but the absence of respect was certainly an exacerbating factor.

Respect is a close relative of tolerance, and both go a long way to prevent and alleviate the negative interactions between and among people. Respect was a member of each Lakota household during the free-roaming buffalo-hunting days on the northern Plains.

After the arrival of the horse, the average Lakota tipi—which means "they live there"—was sixteen to eighteen feet across. Its overall shape was conical, the floor plan was slightly more egg-shaped than circular, and it had only one room. The basic components were twenty to twenty-two soft, tanned, and dehaired bison hides sewn together, which formed the covering. It was supported by sixteen to twenty long, slender poles arranged and lashed together in a cone-shaped framework. At the top was a smoke hole with directional flaps and at the bottom edge was the only door, usually faced to the east. The tipi was perfectly suited to the nomadic lifestyle. Its care and construction and disassembly and reassembly were the exclusive responsibility of the women. They could take it down in less than half an hour and needed no more time than that to put it up at the next encampment.

Inside of this wonderfully appropriate dwelling lived, on the average, seven people. Many households consisted of three generations living in the same dwelling. The use and arrangement of space was critical to the family's harmony, since this was a one-room structure. Amazingly the disputes over space were rare because of one simple and essential presence: respect.

Each member of the household took no more space than he or she needed and, with the possible exception of the children, was careful not to encroach on someone else's space. There was also a simple way to handle the issue of privacy. If a non-Lakota observer was a fly on the wall inside a Lakota tipi as the family was preparing for bed, he or she would probably think that the people in the tipi were rudely ignoring one another. As a point of fact, they would have been, but not out of rudeness. Since there were no interior walls to provide privacy, people politely ignored one another. Frequently, for example, it would seem that the younger husband and wife were totally unaware of the grandparents, and vice versa. But they were simply affording each other privacy. The children, of course, had access to all the adults in the household, but they were nonetheless learning the proper etiquette for a necessary aspect of family life, an etiquette firmly rooted in respect.

Two significant historical events are proof that respect for others, even one's enemies, is certainly possible. The first occurred in 1851 and the second, fifteen years later in 1866.

The Oregon Trail had been firmly established by 1850 as the primary white emigrant route from Missouri to Oregon, a trek of some 2,000 miles. From its jumping-off point in western

Missouri, it followed old, established travel corridors through Kansas, Nebraska, Wyoming, Idaho, and finally Oregon. Over its twenty-year history, 350,000 people would use it.

Through northwest Nebraska and southeast Wyoming, the trail was in Lakota territory, but along its entire route the white emigrants were fearful of Indian attacks. Primarily because of this concern, United States peace commissioners called for a treaty meeting at Fort Laramie, in southeastern Wyoming, and invited many of the tribes from the northern Plains. In the spring of 1851 many of the invitees showed up, including the Lakota, Cheyenne, Arapaho, Mandan, Hidatsa, Arikara, Crow, Shoshoni, and Blackfeet. The Lakota, Cheyenne, and Arapaho had by then formed a strong alliance and had clashed at one time or another with all of the other tribes. There was especially bad blood between the Lakota and Crow, and between the Lakota and Shoshoni as well. But for the entire forty days or so of the treaty gathering there were no clashes. Old enemies set aside their differences for the time being and had a good time at the expense of the United States and its peace commissioners.

The peace commissioners were wholly ignorant of the dynamics and factors that were part and parcel of centuries-old interrelationships of the tribes of the northern Plains, but they knew just enough to be fearful of outbreaks of fighting. Consequently, they paternalistically admonished the attendees against fighting of any kind. When the gathering was conducted and concluded peacefully, the commissioners therefore assumed that the absence of conflict was due to their admonishment. In fact, one of the conditions of the Fort Laramie Treaty of 1851 was that the tribes of the northern Plains were to forever cease and desist from any further intertribal warfare. While tribal representatives signed the treaty, once the gathering ended and they returned to their own territories, old hostilities were resumed. As a matter of fact, many of the tribes had come to Fort Laramie simply out of curiosity and to collect on the promise of goods from the U.S. government—blankets, food, cloth, beads, tools, implements, and so on.

The gathering of tribes at the Horse Creek Council—as the Lakota and other tribes called it—was peaceful for the same reason that several generations of a Lakota family coexisted harmoniously in the same small dwelling: respect. Old enemies who had clashed many times were able to temporarily set aside their animosities.

Fifteen years later and some two hundred miles to the northwest of Fort Laramie, my ancestors accorded respect to a fallen enemy. In disregard of the conditions of another treaty promulgated at Fort Laramie, whites opened a trail through the heart of Lakota country in the Powder River region of what is now north central Wyoming. The Bozeman Trail was a direct route to the gold fields of Montana. The U.S. government further violated its agreement with us by building three forts along the trail and causing an almost continuous conflict for a period of six years that was known as Red Cloud's War. Red Cloud was an Oglala Lakota leader who had been prominent in the Fort Laramie negotiations.

Fort Phil Kearny was built in 1866 a few miles north of the present town of Buffalo, Wyoming, along the eastern slopes of the Big Horn Mountains: the Shining Mountains, as my ancestors called them. Almost from the day the U.S. Army contingent arrived to build the fort, the Lakota harassed them on a regular basis because the whites were there in violation of their promise to seek and obtain Lakota permission to enter the Powder River country. That harassment culminated in a decisive battle on the twenty-first of December. An eighty-man combined force of infantry and cavalry was lured into a trap by ten decoys led by Crazy Horse, who was twenty-five or twenty-six at the time. By the time the soldiers realized they had been led into an ambush, it was too late. A force of five-hundred to seven-hundred Lakota and Northern Cheyenne wiped them out in less than an hour. History books call it the Fetterman Massacre, after the brash

Indian-hating officer who led his entire command to its death. We call it the Battle of the Hundred in the Hand. It was far from a massacre. It was a hard-fought battle in which the soldiers fought fiercely and inflicted heavy casualties.

Toward the end of the fight the Lakota saw one soldier fighting with nothing more than the bugle in his hands. He was killed, of course, but his bravery impressed those who witnessed his determined efforts. Out of respect for his bravery he was not scalped, and one Lakota warrior went so far as to cover his body with a buffalo robe.

Respect, as in the story of the young hunter who resisted the charms of the Deer Woman, can sometimes be a lifesaver. It did save the life of a Crow warrior who managed to sneak into a Lakota camp to steal a horse.

The Crow warrior was young and was eager to prove himself. He had hidden near the Lakota camp and waited for nightfall, knowing that the best war horses and buffalo-hunting horses were tied near the lodge doors for the night. When it was sufficiently dark, he crept into camp and carefully worked his way toward one particular lodge where a tall, black war horse was picketed. He was so skillful and silent that not a single camp dog was aware of his presence as he cut the horse's lead rope. But he was not aware that two Lakota sentinels had spotted him and followed his every move. With bent bows they waited for him to reach the edge of the camp. When he did, they would shoot him and recover the horse.

As the Crow walked as nonchalantly as he could through the camp, an old woman emerged unexpectedly from one of the lodges. She hurried to the woodpile and took up a large armload of wood, so large in fact that she could barely carry it. The young Crow, seeing the old woman's dilemma, immediately went to her aid and carried her firewood for her. He, of course, had a grandmother whom he admired and respected. When he finished his task, he turned to find the two Lakota sentinels waiting with their bent bows with arrows aimed at his chest. Instead of killing him, however, the sentinels recovered the nearly stolen horse, disarmed the Crow, and escorted him a short distance from the village. From there they turned him loose to return to his own village. Respect for the elderly was a common element among all of the tribes of the Plains.

Respect manifests itself in many ways. The Lakota, as well as other Plains tribes, were heavily dependent on the *tatanka,* or bison, for their livelihood. The abundance of bison meant strength and prosperity, and the Lakota were grateful for that wealth. Careful preparations were made before bison hunts, and ceremonies were conducted to ask the bison for the privilege of the taking and use of his flesh. After the hunt the hunters respectfully thanked the animals for the gift of their lives, and asked forgiveness as well. But it didn't end there. As a further demonstration of respect, the Lakota used every piece of the bison. Hides were used for winter robes and tipi coverings. Horns were turned into cups, ladles, and spoons. Sinew—the hamstring cord—was dried and used for thread and bowstring. Hooves were boiled to make glue, and the hair was twisted and made into cord and rope, and the like. Nothing was wasted. As a final act of respect, anytime a Lakota found a bison skull, he or she would be certain it faced the east to meet the rising sun so that the spirit of the animal could be in unison with the rhythm of life.

Respect for all forms of life, unfortunately, is not a common value in many cultures today. It is easier to respect someone stronger, faster, smarter, or richer. Likewise, it is easy to respect someone who is as much like us in every way possible. Respecting someone with different beliefs, different dress, or different customs, or *something* entirely different from us is not easy. Perhaps that is the tragic reason Luther Standing Bear's cautionary sentiments have come to pass.

In December of 1998 thirty-one wild horses were shot and killed in a place called Largomarsino Canyon, a rugged area just east of Reno, Nevada. Details of the killings brought to light by law enforcement investigators ignited local, national, and international outrage. Each of the victims had been shot in the hind legs or the stomach, or both in some cases. Some of the victims were pregnant mares, one of which went into labor after she was wounded but expired before she could completely deliver her foal. Autopsies performed by several local veterinarians corroborated the preliminary evidence. The shooters, it would seem, wanted their victims to experience a painful, lingering death.

Thirty-three horses in all were killed. Thirty-one were found dead in Largomarsino Canyon and two, found shot and badly injured, had to be put down.

Three suspects were arrested and charged, initially with shooting twenty-eight horses. A district judge later ruled that the evidence could support only one charge. The remaining charge amounts to gross misdemeanor and carries a penalty of one year in the county jail and a fine of two thousand dollars.

Regardless of the outcome of this case, the fact remains that wild horses were shot in such a manner to cause a slow, painful death. What would motivate or drive anyone to carry out such a horrific act? Possibly arrogance, a sense of impunity or invincibility, a lust for killing, or perhaps just plain boredom. Perhaps the more relevant question in this case is "What values are lacking in anyone who can kill horses in cold blood?"

A friend of mine wrote of an incident during a hunt in Alaska. He and two companions, all accomplished hunters and guides, had been stalking Dall sheep. Two rams had eluded them, but by sheer luck they managed to surround a third. According to my friend the ram probably had never seen humans in his life, and his initial curiosity turned to confusion. As the three hunters closed in on him, he frantically jumped from rock to rock but had nowhere to go.

My friend wrote of the incident: "Two of my hunting partners and I once came face-to-face with the line that separates hunting from mere killing. In that situation we had a chance to murder a full-curl Dall sheep, but turned down the opportunity. . . . In all my days of bowhunting, I have rarely felt pity for an animal because they usually have all the odds in their favor. But I felt pity for this sheep, and I knew I couldn't shoot him. . . . Had we chosen, I feel certain we could have drawn the net tight and killed him as he jumped frantically around the rocks. Instead, we opened it and let him go with shouts to be more careful next time."

John "Jay" Massey was the name of my friend, a world-class bowhunter and guide as well as a primitive bowyer and arrowsmith. Jay died of cancer in 1996. Though he professes to have felt pity for the Dall ram, what Jay had was a profound respect for everything that was part of the natural environment. He let the ram live because he understood that all life is sacred, and he didn't kill simply because he could.

What separates a Jay Massey from someone who can kill thirty-one horses? The obvious answer is a respect for life, a respect for all living things. And how does one gain or learn that respect? One hopes it is by example: unfortunately, that's how arrogance, hatred, prejudice, and a long list of other undesirable traits are taught and learned as well.

There is a black beetle who lives in our house. He wanders seemingly aimlessly about, but I'm sure he knows where he's going. Perhaps he's looking for a companion because, so far, he's alone. We've named him Bailey and we allow him the run of the place. A time or two I've picked him up and placed him out of the way of our foot traffic. I suppose it would be easy to toss him out into the yard where the blackbirds and magpies are waiting.

Our daughters were curious about Bailey, and one of his appearances elicited a strident "Oh, yuck!" and a few semihorrified screams. But by and large they tolerate him because we adults do. One of them asked if he was still around because he hadn't put in an appearance for several days. Amazingly, he seems to have outwitted the bat that was flying around in our family room a few days ago.

I tried to coax the bat out through an open door, not sure exactly how such a thing could be done. The bat hid someplace in an unreachable crack or crevice in our log house, and my search with a flashlight yielded no clues. Then he or she flapped through our bedroom one night. Putting on work gloves, I tried to catch him or her as he or she cavorted about the room while my wife sensibly retreated beneath the covers. The bat finally alighted on a log wall—head down, of course—and I was able to grab it. The bat was not pleased at the turn of events and let me know in no uncertain terms with a series of low squeals as I tossed him or her out into the night. It would have been just as easy to attack the bat with a fly swatter, but strangely, at the moment I was about to grab it, I felt as though my grandparents were watching. And as I watched the bat fly off into the cool night air and turned to walk back to the bedroom, I felt taller somehow and at peace with the world. It's amazing, and reassuring, what a little respect can do.

What kind of examples influenced the killers of thirty-one horses? It is enough to say that those examples were not remotely associated with respect—and to ask whether any segments of their community or society in general nurtured or encouraged their personal values.

Wild horses have been a part of North America for several hundred years. They number in the thousands and their range is now predominantly public lands in several western states. They've been harassed and killed since about the turn of the century, sometimes directly sanctioned and enabled by the federal government. One mustanger recalls killing as many as eight hundred wild horses in the course of two or three days.

Wild horse herds are in direct competition with domestic livestock for forage and water, and are therefore considered by many ranchers as an expensive nuisance. That kind of local sentiment had to have had some influence on the killers of those thirty-one horses. Perhaps there was outright encouragement or sanction, or perhaps it wasn't necessary. The obvious, long-entrenched negative feelings toward wild horses in some seg-ments of the ranching community could have been regarded as implied support or encouragement. In any case, we are left with the chilling reality that wanton killing of wild horses is not a thing of the past, and that old attitudes are sometimes impossi-ble to change. But even more frightening is the ominous possi-bility that the cold-blooded murder of thirty-one horses is a sign that we have lost the essential virtue in our relationship with anything or anyone we define as different: respect.

Some people regard the killing of thirty-one horses as noth-ing more than a regrettable incident—a symptom of western mentality. Others think it is a violation of the sanctity of life. If there are those among us who can, in cold blood, shoot and kill a form of life obviously regarded not only as different but also inferior, should we be surprised at horrible incidents such as Columbine or the dragging death of Willie Byrd?

At the other end of the spectrum, the practice of respect doesn't grab headlines, but perhaps it should. A rancher strongly opposed to the reintroduction of wolves into Yellowstone Na-tional Park listened as fellow ranchers tried to shout down the person spearheading the effort to put wolves back into the park. With hat in hand he stood and quietly reminded everyone pres-ent that she had just as much right to be heard. When a young marine faces withering enemy gunfire to rescue a fallen com-rade, for whom he has loudly and frequently expressed his dis-like, and is wounded severely in the process, another marine is forced to ask, "Why would you do that for someone you don't like?" To which the grievously wounded Marine replied, "I may not like him, but I respect him."

◇◇◇

My grandparents gave me numerous reasons to respect them for who and what they were, and still are, to me. Because of them the story of Koskalaka and the Deer Woman is especially mean-ingful for me. I've never literally seen the Deer Woman, but she's figuratively crossed my path a time or two. Koskalaka resisted her because of the deep respect he felt for his grandmother, and I certainly can identify with that. But there was an instance in my early childhood when both my grandparents taught me a lesson about respect without saying a word.

They had volunteered to clean an old rural church. We traveled to it in our horse-drawn wagon early one morning and spent the entire day working in the church. We swept the floors, mopped, dusted, and washed windows. That was the least of the chores. A swarm of honeybees had taken up residence in one corner of the building and could obviously be a hazard for any two-legged types.

My grandfather built a small fire near that corner outside of the building and piled green grass on it to create heavy smoke. To my surprise, the smoke drove the bees from their hive, but they were none too happy at the disturbance, and my grandfather was stung several times. Some of the bees found their way inside and collected against the windows. My grandmother gathered them up by hand and released them out the door. Though she was stung a few times, she managed to clear them all out without killing or injuring a single one.

Later, when the priest had learned of what happened, he scolded my grandparents and told them in no uncertain terms that they should have used liberal doses of insecticide to kill the bees. "After all, they are only insects," he said. In more ways than one, that episode had to have been the most painful lesson my grandparents ever taught: a lesson I remember each time I see a honeybee.

Respect for his grandmother certainly did save Koskalaka. Respect enabled Jay Massey to make a choice based on his reverence for life. It enabled enemies to set aside generations of animosity and conflict and live in peace for a time. It enabled warriors to acknowledge the bravery in battle of an enemy, though his kind were especially hated for their arrogance. And it saved the life of a would-be horse thief because it was an innate part of his character.

Of all virtues, respect is arguably the one that consistently creates itself in its own image. My grandmother suffered a stroke while still a young woman. A medicine man came to heal her. He prayed and gave her medicine and told her she would be well again and live a long life. But to remind her to live a good life, Wakantanka—the Great Mystery—would send someone to help her remember. That morning, at sunrise, she opened the door to the sweat lodge and saw that someone—her helper. It was a tiny screech owl, also known as a burrowing owl because it lives with the prairie dogs in their burrows. The screech owl was sitting on a post. My grandmother asked me always to be kind to the screech owls because they were her helpers. I respected them for what they meant to her and I never harmed one.

4

Honor

Wayuonihan (wah-you-o-knee-han)

To have integrity, to have an honest and upright character

✛ The Story of the Snake

The old ones liked to say that there are many strange and mysterious things in this world. They knew this to be true because they had seen things: some wondrous, some funny, some powerful or small. But everything has a purpose, they said, everything that happens is a gift from life itself, if for nothing else than to teach us a lesson.

My grandfather told me about some hunters long ago who met something powerful and mysterious, and learned a lesson about honor. A lesson they would remember each time they saw a snake.

Four hunters went into the great mountains we call *Paha Sapa,* the Black Hills, whose pine-covered slopes look black from a distance. These mountains are important to us because they are so mysterious and powerful, and because the old ones say we came up out of the Earth through a hole in the ground there, a cave. Today it is called Wind Cave.

Hunting was always good in the Black Hills because elk and deer were always plentiful. After a day's travel into the mountains the hunters made camp in a secluded, narrow meadow. There they prepared their weapons and rested. They fell asleep that night, eager for the new day and for good things to happen. Sometime in the night one of them awoke to add wood to the fire and saw a frightening and terrible sight. A giant snake had encircled them and their camp.

The hunter was frightened. He closed his eyes and opened them, but the snake was still there. He woke the others, motioning them to keep silent and pointed at the snake. None of them had ever seen such a thing. It seemed as though they were all having the same bad dream, and all they could do was huddle together in confusion. As yet the snake had not moved.

"What shall we do?" the youngest of them asked in a whisper. "Perhaps we can kill it with arrows if we all shoot at once."

"No!" cautioned the oldest. "If we cannot kill it, it will kill us. It has to be very powerful. We must think of a way to escape while it seems to be asleep."

They stood around the dying fire, but the moonlight through the large pines was bright and they could see red and black stripes on the snake. They waited, each of them expecting the thing to disappear because nothing in their lives had prepared them to believe that giant snakes were real. But it didn't disappear, so they had to believe it was real.

"We must do something!" one of them said. "If it is asleep, it will certainly eat us when it awakens! It could swallow us all easily!"

Without a doubt it could. Its back was as high as the hump of a buffalo, and it was as long as twenty buffalo standing in a circle nose to tail.

"There is only one thing to do," the oldest hunter told them. "We must jump over it."

All of them were strong and healthy, but none of them had ever had to jump over a giant snake.

"We can dig a hole, get in, and cover ourselves," suggested another. "Perhaps it will think we have escaped, and leave."

"The ground is full of stones," said the oldest. "We have no tools to dig such a large hole. We must jump before it wakes."

The others yielded to that logic, though not without some misgivings. Clearly, the one place to jump over was where the snake's head and tail came together, because it was the lowest spot.

"First we must throw our bows and arrows over," said the oldest hunter, who was the leader. "I will go last and you must be first," he said to the youngest. "Take a run and leap over that spot where the head and tail are."

"I cannot," whined the young man. "What if I cannot jump high enough, or if I fall?"

"It is more than likely certain that the snake is here to eat us," said the leader, "so you must try." He tossed his weapons a good distance into the trees, over the snake's back, as did the others. But the youngest was too frightened to jump so the leader pointed to the next man. "Go. Take a run and jump!"

The man stepped back just beyond the fire as the others moved aside to give him room. Suddenly he dashed forward and jumped, tumbling over the snake's head and into the brush beyond. He landed with a thud and stood, motioning for the others to follow. Encouraged, the next man did likewise, crashing through the brush at the edge of the trees behind the snake.

The leader grabbed the youngest hunter by the shoulders. "See," he said, "it can be done. They have jumped and you can, too."

The young man took deep breaths. "Yes," he said uncertainly. "I will try." Then he stepped beyond the fire, tried not to look at the snake, and ran as hard as he could.

He might have made it. His fear had helped him jump so high he would have cleared the snake's back, but he didn't because the snake raised his head and sent the young man crashing back to the ground near the fire. He landed so hard he was knocked out.

The two hunters who had already jumped ran and hid in the trees. The leader quickly bent over the unconscious young hunter as the snake raised its terrible head and stared at them with unblinking eyes. There was nothing to be done. The two hunters were at the mercy of something they didn't know existed, until that night.

Frightened down to the core of his very being, the leader could do nothing but await what might happen. After a long wait, all the while chilled by the unblinking black eyes of the giant snake, he felt the young man stir. Strangely, the snake moved at the same time, crawling off into the dark forest, silently moving through the trees in spite of its size. When it was gone, the other hunters came out of hiding. The youngest one woke and grabbed his head.

"I have a terrible headache," he said, "the snake spoke to me in my head."

The other two hunters gathered their weapons and strung their bows. "It might come back," one of them said. "If it does, we must fight it!"

"No!" said the youngest, "it will not come back."

"What do you mean?" asked the leader.

"The snake talked to me, inside my head," said the youngest. "It has asked us to do something for him. If we do not, he will find us and swallow us."

The others thought for a moment. Perhaps there was something to what the young one was saying. After all, before tonight none of them would have believed that such a thing as a giant snake was real. So that same giant snake talking to the young man in his head was not difficult to believe.

"What did the snake tell you?" asked one.

"We must make a journey north by east," he told them, "until we come to a flat river and follow it into a low valley. There we will find a single lodge with a red door. A man lives there with his wife and child, a man with a scar under his eye; he will be expecting us. Two of us must wait with the wife and child while the other two take the man north, keeping north by east, across the Great Muddy River and on until they find a long, narrow lake that is not deep. The man must walk across that lake. The snake said if he crosses to the other side, he will be free to return home."

"If he does not cross to the other side, what will happen?" the leader asked.

"I do not know," replied the young man. "I know only that the man must walk into that lake and try to reach the other side. Whatever happens, we must return to his lodge."

They stayed awake the rest of the night, afraid that the snake would return. But it didn't. In the morning they traveled east and by sundown they were out of the mountains. The following sunrise they headed north by east and two days later they came to a river and camped.

"Are you certain the snake talked to you?" asked one of the hunters. "Could it be that you thought he did? Perhaps it was only a dream."

"Was the snake a dream?" asked the leader. "I have never heard of such a thing. Yet I saw it. Am I to think my eyes and ears were lying to me?"

"I am only trying to be certain we are not being led into a dangerous thing," replied the first hunter, "or made to look like fools. I, for one, think that traveling into country we don't know, perhaps even into enemy country, because we listened to someone who said a snake talked to him is laughable."

"I have not lied," insisted the youngest hunter. "I told you what I heard! The snake said if we do not do as he says, he will take us all; he will swallow us!"

"You are free to go," the leader said to the first hunter. "You do not have to believe what this young man says. But, remember, we all saw the snake! We all saw what happened to this young man. So I believe him because I don't want a giant snake following me, waiting to swallow me!"

"If we find the lone lodge with a red door," retorted the first hunter, "then we will know this is all true. If we do not find such a lodge or a man with a scar below his eye, I will go home, back to doing something sensible!"

The next day, after following the river for half a day, they came to a valley. Not too far into the valley they came upon a lodge in a grove of trees. The lone lodge had a red door. In it lived a man with a young wife and a child. The man had a scar under one eye.

The hunters were more surprised to see him than he was to see them, as if he knew they were coming. The man was past middle age with streaks of gray in his hair, and his wife was very young. He showed them a good spot along the river for their camp and lingered to talk.

"My wife will have food for you. You must come to my lodge and eat. You have traveled far, and I knew that you would come some day," he told them. "I know also that you have something to tell me."

The hunters were reluctant, but they had been given a task. So the leader revealed the purpose of their journey. "Two of us are to remain with your wife and child while two take you north by east, across the Great Muddy River and on to a long, shallow lake. It is many, many days journey, perhaps as much as one moon. When we reach that lake, you are to walk across. If you reach the other shore, you can come home."

"Yes," said the man with the scar under his eye, "I will travel with you. We can leave two days from now. I wish to have one more day with my wife and son before I—before I must leave. When you have made your camp, come to our lodge and eat."

First a giant snake and now a mysterious man with a scar. The hunters didn't know what to think. For certain they had been drawn into something they knew nothing about, and a long, long journey into unknown territory awaited them.

"Why must he walk across that lake?" asked one of the hunters as they made camp.

"Why does he live here with only his wife and child?" asked the second hunter. "Was he banished from a village? Only people who are banished live alone."

"If he is banished, what did he do?" wondered the leader. "It was more than likely something very bad. A man is not banished for something minor."

The evening meal of elk stew, prepared and served by the man's young wife, was very good. She was courteous and very shy. Her baby was just now walking and stayed close to his mother after the strangers entered his home. The four hunters were polite guests, and very grateful for a woman's cooking.

The talk around the fire was about hunting and about the good late summer weather. Nothing was said about the arrival of the hunters, or the news they brought. The evening passed pleasantly and soon the hunters excused themselves, not wanting to overstay the hospitality of the cozy lodge.

They spent the next day resting and making arrows. The leader decided that he and the youngest hunter should accompany the man north: a decision not disputed by the other two. Much of their talk was about the man with the scar under his eye, who as yet offered no explanation for his situation. They sensed that he was a good man, but they also saw a quiet sadness about him. That evening he came to their camp.

"My wife knows I must make this journey with you," he said. "She wants to accompany me. We have not been apart since we became husband and wife. It is hard for her, this thing that I must do. But she will wait, as she knows she must."

"These two will stay," said the leader, pointing to two of his companions. Indicating the remaining hunter, he said, "He and I will travel with you because the snake talked to him. And because when I was a younger man I traveled into that north country. It is the home of our enemies, so we must be careful."

"I, too, went north as a young man," said the man with the scar. "I crossed the Great Muddy, but it was in winter. I shall be ready at dawn, and we will go."

Once again the man had not given an explanation.

"You must be cautious," advised one of the hunters who was staying. "You will be in enemy country, but more than that there is something about this that we don't know. It is not good to be blind about anything."

At dawn the three men departed. The young wife stood at the door of her lodge and watched until she could no longer see the travelers.

Ten days brought them to the Great Muddy River. It was late summer and the powerful river was low, though it still took all of their strength to cling to a log and swim with it across to the other shore. After several more days they were into enemy territory.

The flat, wide-open prairie country can make wanderers out of any being, whether it walks, crawls, or flies. The openness, one low hill after another, beckons. The top of one hill lures one to the next to see what is beyond. The three travelers saw great herds of the white-bellied goats—the antelope—and even greater herds of buffalo that covered the land like a great brown cloud. Above them soared the hawks and eagles and the buzzards and ravens. If not for the uncertainty that awaited them at the end of their journey, the joy they felt at being part of the Earth would not seem so out of place.

Around the evening campfires the man with the scar had talked easily but revealed little of himself—nothing at all to point to the reason for this strange journey. As yet he had said nothing of the snake, nor did he ask a question. The only certainty—as the snake had said—was that the man had been expecting the hunters to come to his lodge. And every night he had gone off a distance from the camp to smoke his pipe and pray.

In enemy country they traveled more slowly, keeping out of sight in the valleys. Fifteen days after crossing the Great Muddy River, they came to a long lake that curved much like a new moon. Though they had passed by several lakes, big and small, they knew this lake was the one. There was something here; the hunters could sense it. And there were no animals and no birds in the sky or near the water. There was only a strange silence.

Since entering enemy country they had made few fires, and now they made a cold camp in a hidden cove at the water's edge. The two hunters were watchful for enemies, yet they knew somehow that none would come. "There is something about this place," the leader said. "There is a feeling here."

"Yes," said the young hunter, "the same feeling when I first saw the snake."

The man with the scar had spoken not at all since they had found the lake. That evening he went off alone. In a while they could hear him singing his death song. As the moon rose he returned and spoke to his companions.

"Tomorrow, after sunrise, I will walk into the lake, as you told me I must do. I think I know what awaits me, in the water. If I do not reach the other shore, take my things home to my wife. Be so kind as to see her back to her family. She has been away from them for too long. Ask her, also, what you want to know about me. She will tell you." So saying, he went away to sit near the water to await the dawn.

The two hunters were certain of one thing. The man with the scar on his face was brave.

Dawn came and turned into a pale red glow over the east horizon, and the waters of the lake shimmered with the same pale glow. Soon the sun rose over the edge of the Earth. The hunters watched as the man with the scar removed his shirt and leggings, standing only in his breechclout and moccasins. Singing his death song, and without looking back, he entered the water.

There was no wind; the lake was calm and flat as though frozen. A strange silence filled the air as the man walked farther and farther into the lake. It was shallow. Even as he drew near to the middle the water reached only to his thigh. The hunters stood on the shore and watched, hoping and praying that the man would reach the other shore.

The width of the lake was more than an arrow could fly from

a strong bow, but they could see the other shore. When the man reached the middle the water rose to his chest. It was then that something happened behind him. There was motion; the water began to move as if boiling. Something dark broke the surface for just a heartbeat; then the man with the scar on his face was taken under.

The hunters ran up and down the shoreline as the waters of the lake once more became calm and flat. It was as if nothing had happened. They knew in their hearts that the man was gone, but they waited, hoping. The morning passed; there was nothing, only the strange silence. Sadly they gathered up his shirt and leggings, his bow and arrows, and his lance and began their journey home.

Twenty days passed before they returned to the lodge with the red door standing in the valley of the flat river. The two waiting hunters were happy for their return.

"Some time ago, many days," one said, "she began to weep and gashed her arms in mourning, and cut her hair. And since then she has worn ashes on her face."

"She knows something," said the leader. "She knows her husband is gone. He did not reach the other shore of that lake. Something pulled him under."

The youngest hunter gave the man's belongings to his mourning wife. She took them and thanked him for taking the journey with her husband. They waited for days out of respect for her state of mourning, making sure that she had food and water. One day she finally spoke to them.

"I must return to my village," she said.

"We will take you there; your husband asked us to do so, and we will," said the leader.

They traveled south by east and the young widow spoke not at all. Though she cooked for them and would help set up their night camps, she kept her thoughts to herself. After fifteen days they came to a large encampment just west of the Great Muddy River, north of where the Bad River flows into it.

She was welcomed home by her family. The hunters were invited to stay as long as they chose, but they were anxious to return to their homes. They did stay to rest for a few days.

On the evening before they were to leave, the young widow came to the hunters' camp. "I must tell you of my husband," she said. "When he was a young man, he had a good friend who became a powerful medicine man. But he turned to the darker side of the powers he had and became a helper for some bad spirits. My husband turned away from him, and in time he became a great warrior and a leader to whom the people turned. The medicine man was jealous of that and used his powers against my husband. He used a special medicine to take my husband's first wife away from him. Even then my husband would not give in, and the medicine man was shamed in front of the people. He went crazy and died that way.

"A spirit, a bad spirit, came to my husband. He said there was to be punishment but that my husband had to choose. He could take the shame of banishment or he could watch his own village go crazy like the medicine man did. My husband chose banishment. The spirit told him that one day four men would come for him, but that he would never know when. The spirit wanted my husband to think that every day was his last. He had one other choice. My husband could lift the punishment from himself whenever he wanted, but that meant his whole village would go crazy."

"How is it that you became his wife?" the youngest hunter asked.

"My father sent me to him," she replied. "He told me the story of this brave and honorable man, and said that his kind of honor and bravery must not die with him. It must be passed on. And so it has because I have his child."

The hunters returned to their own village. When their relatives asked why they had been away for so long, they would only reply that they had lost their way and made a long journey. But in time they told the story of that long journey. Some of the people believed it and some did not. Yet over time it was noticed that the four hunters who shared the journey were the humblest and most honorable men in the village.

Perhaps it is difficult to believe in giant snakes, but I have lived long enough to know that there is much I don't know. I can't say for certain that giant snakes don't exist because I have seen many things in my life that may seem unbelievable to some or just normal to others: like a man walking on the moon. But I do know for certain that there are many wondrous, powerful, and mysterious things we may experience in our lives. I hope one of them is honor.

The Color of Honor

A wise man was asked what virtue he would choose if he were to be known by only one. "Honor," he replied without hesitation. "If I am known for being honorable, it can only mean that I have demonstrated many other virtues."

The application of virtue is the positive core of any culture, society, or nation. Like individuals, nations can be kind, generous, truthful, honest, generous, and courageous. Those individuals, cultures, societies, and nations that indiscriminately—blindly, if you will—apply all virtues in their conduct and dealings will establish themselves and emerge as the most honorable. To be honorable is to have integrity—to be honest—and to do what is morally correct. As much as judgment is based on what we do, it is also, and perhaps more indelibly, defined by what we fail to do.

A man received as payment more money than he was owed. He kept the extra sum, looking on it as an unexpected reward. But the values he was taught told him that it was wrong to have kept the extra money. For many years he pushed aside that truth, but it remained in his awareness like a pebble in his shoe. Finally he returned twice the amount of the extra money and was highly commended for it, but he was circumspect and turned aside all the praise. "Don't you feel good about your honorable act?" he was asked. "No," he replied, "returning the money after all these years was merely atonement. The honorable act would have been to return it immediately."

Honor was, and is, important to Lakota culture just as it is to cultures the world over. But to define the traditional Lakota sense of honor it is necessary to examine Plains Indian intertribal warfare.

It is perhaps incongruous or illogical to speak of honor within the context of warfare and combat given the terrible efficiency of modern weaponry and the horrific record of wartime atrocities. Any extremely difficult situation demands courage, and war and combat are arguably the most extreme tests of courage. As despicable as war is, it is a saving grace for the human species that most who engage or participate in it endeavor to do so with honor. Honor can be as simple as a cease-fire when the vanquished lay down their arms. It can be as grandiose as General Ulysses Grant allowing the surrendering Confederate soldiers to keep their horses at the end of the American Civil War in 1865. Among the Plains Indian tribes prior to the so-called Indian Wars of the nineteenth century, honor was often associated with warfare for practical and moral reasons.

War is, and has been, basically the same the world over. If it is defensive action, it is usually to resist encroachment or invasion—imperialism. As an offensive action it is usually to encroach or invade, which are imperialistic notions. Consequently, a nation or a culture is judged by how and why it engaged itself in war. Intertribal warfare on the pre-European Plains of North America was perceived to be rooted in savagery first and foremost simply because the people of the Plains were considered to be savages. Savage is as savage does. However, intertribal warfare had a different meaning and purpose than the usual defensive-offensive aspects of imperialistic warfare. It was in a real sense an intentional proving ground.

Lakota fighting men achieved honors in the arena of combat from courageous deeds and honorable conduct. Armed clashes between enemy tribes were rarely long, arduous campaigns involving hundreds of warriors. They were more often intense, short-lived engagements between small forces of ten to fifty men. And while it was necessary to protect home, family, and precious hunting territories, warfare as a consequence of outright imperialism was infrequent. More frequent was the provocation of conflict solely to create an opportunity for combatants to conspicuously display deeds of courage and honor.

There was one highly significant difference between European-style warfare and Plains Indian warfare. Europeans and Euro-Americans fought to kill as many of the enemy as possible while doing considerable damage to their supplies and support functions. Plains Indian warriors endeavored to demonstrate courage and honor in the face of the enemy, and defeating an enemy didn't necessarily mean having to kill him. Lakota and other Plains warriors considered it far more courageous, and therefore more honorable, to touch a live enemy in battle and live to tell about it because that courage and honor were the basis for the strength of a tribe. It was "good, strong medicine" to have more of both than the enemy. And it was the number and frequency of brave and honorable deeds that served to defeat one's enemy, not the number of dead bodies on the battlefield. Defeating the enemy in his own mind was better than taking his life.

The unavoidable consequences of combat were wounds and death, always a clear and present danger. Combat was by no means an easy proving ground. There was, therefore, no higher calling than to defend one's people, no greater sacrifice than to lay down one's life in the defense of one's people. That philosophy was summed up in the reminder from the antiquities of memory spoken by women to their husbands and sons to "go boldly ahead, for it is better to lie a warrior naked in death than to be wrapped up well with a heart of water inside." The words of many warrior songs articulate that quite clearly, such as the following:

I go forward under the banner of the people.
I do this so that the people may live.

The underlying rationale was that if a man was capable of acting bravely and honorably in the midst of the most violent, chaotic, and frightening of circumstances, he was capable of bravery and honor in the time of peace. The benefit to the people was twofold. Their fighting men were totally committed to the defense of families, home, and homeland, and the lessons of courage and honor learned under the most difficult of circumstances would serve to benefit all of the people in any circumstance.

Fighting men who gained fame and won honors in the arena of combat achieved high standing in the community. Furthermore, if their leadership under fire led to military successes because of steadiness and wise decision making, they were sought after for civilian leadership where that hard-won experience could be put to use for the benefit of all the people.

In a way, then, warfare was a necessary part of the overall culture, but not in the sense that it was created or used to fulfill a need for violence or aggression. Whether by design or not, a negative aspect of human interaction was used as a vehicle for positive influence.

In the very early 1800s, sometime after the various Plains tribes acquired firearms to some extent, a group of enemy raiders—perhaps Pawnee—made an incursion into Sicangu Lakota territory from the south. The southern boundary then was the Running Water River, now known as the Niobrara River, in what is now north central Nebraska. They managed to advance north nearly to the Smoking Earth (Little White) River before they were detected and pursued. Badly outnumbered, the only recourse for the raiders was to run back south. A relentless pursuit by Sicangu Lakota warriors wore out the enemy horses and forced their riders to make a stand on high ground, a pine-covered knoll on a ridge east of the Smoking Earth River. A few of the raiders had been wounded in the pursuit, and they apparently died of their wounds after a defensive position was established. A siege ensued wherein the Sicangu attempted several charges to dislodge the raiders. A Sicangu was wounded and a horse was killed in the futile attempts. During the night the raiders attempted to break out, but they were turned back and suffered more casualties. The following day saw a series of Sicangu assaults and enemy counterattacks. The Sicangu then decided to wait it out, because they had access to water and plenty of food, not to mention reinforcements. In spite of the dire circumstances, the raiders showed no signs of weakness. They defended themselves bravely and skillfully. Both sides knew that it was only a matter of time before the raiders were out of water and food and ammunition for their two firearms. The Sicangu talked of setting brush fires and forcing the enemy from the hill, but it was decided to let the raiders live because they were brave men.

The leader of the Sicangu contingent signaled for a parley and then met with the leader of the raiders. Through hand signs (a necessary and effective method of communication used by many Plains tribes who couldn't speak each other's language), the offer of clemency was made, likewise the reply. The raiders surrendered their horses in return for safe passage to the south bank of the Running Water River. Their dead, buried in shallow graves atop the pine-covered ridge, were to be left unmolested.

My grandfather told me this story. He also said that war is really a fight between the good and the bad sides of humans, and while both emerge during hostilities, it is within each person to choose to bring out the best or the worst part of himself. In this story the Sicangu, I'm proud to say, brought out the best part of themselves.

Interestingly, in the mid 1980s highway engineers digging core samples prior to new highway construction discovered human bones on a ridge top a few miles east of the Little White River and eleven miles west of the town of Mission, South Dakota, on the Rosebud Sioux Indian Reservation. After conferring with Rosebud Sioux (Sicangu Lakota) tribal leaders and elders, the survey line for the new highway bed was moved and the bones remained undisturbed. There is no conclusive evidence that identifies those bones, but in my mind, at least, they are a testament to honor, to man's humanity to man.

I shudder to think of a society where there is absence of honor. The consequences of such a condition would be confusion, chaos, and anarchy. The fine line we walk was drawn because honor cannot be mandated; therefore we are dependent on the ability of individuals, societies, cultures, and nations to choose between the best or the worst part of themselves. Individual choices can be simple or more complicated.

In 1996, in a rural community where we lived, my wife stopped at a convenience store to purchase gasoline. She had only five dollars and managed to go five cents over her limit before she shut off the gas pump. The attendant in the store summarily confiscated her car keys after my wife reported her unintended faux pas. She telephoned to advise me of her predicament and had to wait while I drove to the store to pay the nickel overage. Several months later we moved to a small community in the northwest. I purchased a part for my pickup truck at an auto parts store and was a dollar short. The owner, who didn't know my name or my address or phone number, made up the difference and said I could settle up with him the next time I was in town.

A developer hired an architect, his daughter's fiancé, to design a house for a special client. The house needed to be the architect's best effort, the developer said, a statement of design, function, and beauty. Within a few months the young architect delivered a set of plans to his prospective father-in-law. The man approved the plans and then asked the architect to supervise the construction of the house, giving him complete control and a generous budget.

The young man took the job eagerly. The plans he had drawn were the best he had ever produced, and he was anxious see the house become a reality. He took bids from several construction firms and hired the lowest bidder with the least amount of experience, ignoring the fact that the next lowest bidder had a reputation for completing projects on time and under budget. Next he went to a local lumber yard and purchased the cheapest building materials, saving money but seriously sacrificing quality.

The builder's inexperience resulted in serious structural flaws. Rather than correct them and incur more costs, the architect decided that no one would know the difference once the floors, walls, and ceilings were in place, and he would save money. Outwardly the house was a showpiece. Though its appearance was aesthetically pleasing, the architect was well aware of its hidden weaknesses, but he was just as convinced that the occupants of the house would never know the difference.

The developer arrived with his daughter and accepted the keys to the new house and praised the young architect for a job well done. Then he turned the keys over to the young couple. It was his wedding present to them.

Honor is probably the most difficult virtue to uphold because it requires that one first be honest with oneself. If you can overlook or live with your own dishonor, then it's a simple matter to think that the rest of the world can also.

In the old days a certain warrior society called the Ogle Lute Wicapi, or the Red Shirt Warriors, issued only two invitations for new members once every four years. It was a prestigious club and many wanted to join. But not everyone who was invited was able to pass the test required for membership. It's interesting that those who failed ultimately turned out to be among the most honorable men around.

To earn membership in the Red Shirt Warriors Society, each invitee was asked to face a test of endurance. Without food and water and only a knife for protection, he was required to run a particular route to a well-known landmark—a high shale cliff along a river—climb it, and, then recover a red sash tied to a stone. This was to be done immediately after the new moon in the Middle Moon (July), the hottest time of the year. The only other condition was a time limit of four days. The two invitees would draw lots to determine who would go first.

The prospective member would usually return by sunset of the fourth day: exhausted, hungry, and most of all, thirsty. Before he could take food or water, he was escorted into the lodge of the Red Shirt Warriors Society and asked to present the sash he recovered. In all its history no prospective member had ever failed to return with a red sash. The sash was rolled tightly and the man who brought it back was asked to hold it above his head and let it unfurl. If it extended all the way to the ground, the man had gained membership. If it did not reach the ground, he was denied.

The test was one of physical endurance, but it was also a test of honor. There were two sashes. One was tied to a stone at the top of the shale cliff, and when it was unfurled from above a man's head, it easily reached the ground. The other sash was tied to a tree located at a point just over half way along the route, at a place where it was logical to rest briefly in the shade. That sash was the shorter of the two. If a man unfurled this sash before the elders of the Red Shirt Warriors Society, it was clearly evident that he had not gone the full distance. Those who returned with the short sash were turned away, and the elders of the Society never needed to explain their decision. No one ever received a second invitation to join, but in all its history the few men who were denied membership into the Red Shirt Warriors Society never failed to demonstrate honor in all their undertakings.

In Lakota culture red is the color of honor.

5

Love

Cantognake (chan-doe-gnan-keh)

To place and hold in one's heart

✚ The Story of the Cottonwoods

Cottonwood trees can be found along the rivers and creeks in Lakota country. They are tall and strong and live long lives. In midsummer the breezes play with their leaves, rustling and rattling them until they sing soft, joyful songs that everyone—four-leggeds, wingeds, crawlers, and two-leggeds—likes to hear: songs that can soothe a troubled mind, soften even the hardest heart, or heal a broken one. This is the story of two cottonwood trees who began their lives as something else.

Many, many winters before the white man's steamboat brought the running-face sickness (smallpox) up the Great Muddy River and killed off almost two thousand Lakota in the year 1837, two young people met at a summer gathering. She had just gone through her woman's ceremony and he had counted his first victory against an enemy. She had beautiful dark eyes and he was straight and tall.

They couldn't keep their eyes off one another. Many evenings he stood with her in the soft folds of an elk hide courting robe, just outside her family's lodge, as her mother kept a watchful eye. Hidden beneath the robe the young couple exchanged soft kisses and whispered promises. And at the dances, when the rabbit and round-dance songs were sung, she would pull him into the dancing circle. They would dance side by side, moving together step for step as if they were one person, their gentle voices blending in song with the softly pounding drums.

Everyone could see that the hearts of these two young people were only for each other, and the old people marveled at how their two voices together seemed to rise as one. It was only a matter of time, everyone was certain, before White Lance would take a gift of horses to the family of Red Willow Woman to ask for her hand in marriage.

The summer gathering ended and the two young people re luctantly parted. White Lance rode away with a promise that he would gather many horses.

Summer passed and autumn came. Red Willow Woman's village was encamped near Turtle Butte while White Lance's people were many days' ride to the north near the White Earth River. He had ridden with several war parties against the Arikara and the Crow and distinguished himself by fighting bravely. On one raid he single-handedly captured twelve horses that, of course, were part of the bride price for Red Willow Woman's family.

Leaves turned color and were falling when her village moved just north of the sandhill country to hunt buffalo. It was there that White Lance found them. He and two friends drove eigh-teen horses into the encampment. But his soaring heart fell to earth like a wounded duck, his dreams crushed by Red Willow Woman's own words.

With tears flowing she told him. She had been promised to a young man named He Crow. He was from a respected family and she was honor bound to do her father's bidding.

White Lance had never known such a feeling. The pain in his heart took his breath away; he could not think clearly and his very spirit seemed to curl up inside of him like a lost child. Out of shame and confusion he sent his friends away and rode aimlessly for several days and nights before he returned north. Back in his own village he hid in his mother's lodge and would not eat for days.

In the spring came word that He Crow and Red Willow Woman had been wed. When he heard that, White Lance took his pain and frustration on the warpath against the Crow. On the battlefield he acted recklessly, not seeming to care whether he lived or died.

He Crow, meanwhile, learned that while Red Willow Woman was everything a wife should be and their lodge was always neat and orderly, her heart and mind seemed to be elsewhere. The following spring a daughter was born, but that only seemed to divert Red Willow Woman's attention even more. To cover his disappointment, He Crow rode out often to hunt and accepted every invitation to take to the warpath.

Time passed; many winters came and went. White Lance and Red Willow Woman saw each other once every four seasons at the summer gatherings. Both of them knew that everyone was watching and acted with the utmost propriety, though it was plain to anyone who knew of their situation before that nothing, not even time, could weaken what they truly felt in their hearts.

In time White Lance took a wife, Good Medicine, the widow of a friend killed during a buffalo hunt. He became father to her son, but she understood that while he was a good provider and a dutiful husband, his heart would always belong to another.

More winters passed and White Lance won many war honors, and many men rode with him when he led. He was sought after as a man who gave wise counsel, and he became a leader in peace as well as war. But many, including Good Medicine, saw that he was alone often. In those moments he was seen to be staring off, as if into another time or another place.

Like every good Lakota mother, Red Willow Woman was devoted to her children, for now she had a son as well. But she, too, whiled away many quiet moments, staring off to the north, especially during summer evenings.

White Lance and Red Willow Woman seemed to live for the summer gatherings, when they would have a chance to talk for a few moments. Each asked politely after the other's welfare and how it was with their families, but in their eyes a light would shine and they both seemed to come alive.

Neither White Lance nor Red Willow Woman dishonored their marriages or acted contrary to what was expected of them. The price of honor was to give up true happiness. And each had paid the price with heartbreak. But He Crow and Good Medicine had paid a price as well; it had not been easy for either of them. During one summer gathering He Crow sent word to Good Medicine. They met secretly and talked.

That autumn, long after the summer gathering ended and when the villages had finished their buffalo hunts to make meat for the winter, Good Medicine asked White Lance to take her to visit her relatives, who were encamped to the south. Likewise, He Crow announced his plans to visit relatives to the north and invited Red Willow Woman to accompany him.

The morning after the first night of the new moon, both couples left their villages. They traveled alone because all their children were now grown. After several days White Lance and Good Medicine arrived at a certain place near the Smoking Earth River, a place where hunters often camped along Horse Creek. Good Medicine said she wanted to camp there for a few days.

He Crow and Red Willow Woman arrived a day later. It was awkward, but the couples were happy to see one another. Near the end of that first evening, as cool breezes crawled along from the northwest warning of a hard winter coming, He Crow did a strange thing.

As they all sat in the light of a crackling fire, he tossed a stick to the ground and spoke to Red Willow Woman.

"That stick is you," he said. "I cast you away. You know that in our ways a Lakota husband can cast away his wife by doing so. I have my reasons for this, and now you are away from me; you are free to go where you choose."

Red Willow Woman was stunned. Before she could speak, Good Medicine also did a strange thing. She brought White Lance's belongings out of her lodge and placed them on the ground near the door.

"I give you your things," she said to White Lance. "There is no longer a place for them in my lodge. You know this to be a Lakota woman's right, to cast out her husband in this manner. I have my reasons. You are free to go where you choose."

White Lance was stunned. After a moment he and Red Willow Woman understood what was happening.

"You are the man in her heart," said He Crow to White Lance. "You should be the man in her life, and you shall be."

"And you are the woman in his heart," Good Medicine said to Red Willow Woman. "Take your rightful place with him, as you should have been allowed to do long ago. You have both done your duty, now you must follow your hearts."

The next morning Good Medicine took down her lodge, and He Crow promised to see her safely to her relatives. That night White Lance and Red Willow Woman came together as man and wife twenty-five winters after they had first met.

They lingered in the valley of the Smoking Earth River for days, walking along the river even as the last leaves of autumn floated to the Earth. The world seemed new to them. The sky never looked so blue and the call of the high-flying geese no longer sounded like a sad song. Like the sun chasing away shadows, every new moment together chased off the memories of what should have been. Their hearts soared like hawks on the winds.

The first cold gusts of winter chased them to the sheltering gullies near the Great Muddy River. There they pitched their lodge and White Lance hunted so they could make meat for their journey to Swift Bear's village, many long days to the northwest.

One afternoon he returned from the hunt to find the lodge empty, the ashes in the fire pit cold. Red Willow Woman was nowhere to be seen, and her horse was gone, too. With a little daylight left for tracking, a worried White Lance grabbed his weapons and set out. It was not long before he found her footprints over a set of hoof prints. From the tracks it was plain that Red Willow Woman was trailing her horse. Snow began to fall, lightly at first, as he followed their tracks. As the afternoon wore on the snow became thicker and thicker.

Soon White Lance could no longer see any tracks. He began to call out her name, shouting over and over again. Daylight was fading; he knew it was nearly sundown. The snow covered the ground and hid the sky; there was nothing but whiteness. Then he heard a faint cry, a voice carried by the wind.

White Lance ran toward the sound, and soon dark shapes appeared out of the whiteness and his heart pounded like a fast drum. One of them was Red Willow Woman, huddled on the ground, the snow beneath her red with blood. Over her stood an angry and powerful bear with blood on his claws, roaring as it turned to face White Lance.

As a cry of anguish and rage like an angry summer thunderclap rose from his chest, White Lance ran and thrust his lance. It went true and pierced the animal's great chest, but the beast was powerful and he fought back. It's sharp claws slashed and slashed until White Lance was covered in his own blood. But he stabbed with the lance again and again, piercing the bear's chest each time. The snow turned red with their blood and the cold air was filled with their bellows of rage and pain.

They fell almost at the same heartbeat, the great bear finally weakened by a final thrust of the lance deep into his heart. But he had ripped open the throat of his killer.

With the last remaining heartbeats of life, White Lance crawled to Red Willow Woman and took her in his arms. She summoned her waning strength to pull him close. And so they walked into eternity together as husband and wife.

Two summers were to pass before a group of hunters found the bones near the shore of the Great Muddy River. Two skeletons were entangled. Nearby lay the bleached bones of a bear, the point of a lance embedded inside its ribs. It was not difficult for the hunters to imagine what had happened. They also saw two cottonwood saplings growing side by side in a grassy slope near the water, as if growing from the same root.

Their families placed the bones of White Lance and Red Willow Woman on the same scaffold. As the years passed the saplings grew into tall, sturdy trees, their upper branches twisting around each other like hands interlocking fingers.

As more seasons and years passed, people would come to sit under the two cottonwoods, and in their cool shade they told the story of two young people: she with dark, beautiful eyes and he who stood straight and tall. And as the story was told, the breezes rustled the leaves of the two cottonwoods until they sounded like two gentle voices blending in song, two voices that rose as one.

Several years ago I went to the Great Muddy River, now called the Missouri. I went there alone. I had lost someone dear to me, a friend whose own life was only just beginning when it was taken from her. I walked those shores and watched the rolling waters and recalled the story of the woman with the dark beautiful eyes and her warrior who stood straight and tall. In a grove of young cottonwoods I rested in the shade. There was no way to know if I was near the spot where the two cottonwoods had stood, but I had heard that long after the two trees had fallen and were taken back into the Earth, their stumps could be seen. I found no stumps, but I could hear all around me the rustling leaves of the young cottonwoods coaxed by gentle breezes; and I thought I could hear voices singing. Perhaps it was only my broken heart yearning for comfort, but it was easy to imagine that these young cottonwoods were the children of those two who stood so long ago. My heart wanted to believe it because there was something soothing, something full of promise in the songs of those young cottonwoods.

✚ The Story of the Flutemaker

Beneath the low branches of an old cedar he awoke to a cool breeze caressing his face. For a moment Cloud wondered where he was, and why. Then he remembered what had brought him to this grassy bed beneath the cedar, and the pain of remembering took his breath away.

"My father has accepted the gifts brought by Hollow Horn," Dawn Woman had told Cloud after he had waited for an entire evening by the trail to the river. "Hollow Horn is a fine man and a good provider. He will take good care of me."

"But you are always in my thoughts. You have been in my heart since we were small children. Have you forgotten the promises we made to each other?" he had pleaded.

"We were only children," she had replied. "And what is the promise of a boy against the harshness of life?"

"My promise is everything I have," he had said. "There was a time it made your heart fly. And you cannot tell me that the thought of me will not do so again and again."

Cloud had watched as Dawn Woman walked away into the twilight, soon to be the wife of Hollow Horn. Driven by a cold, sickening pain that shriveled his very being, he had crossed the river and run across the prairies. Trying to outrun the pain in his heart, he ran until his legs drained of all their strength, and all he could do was roll beneath a tree. Only with sleep did the pain subside. But now it returned like a raging flood.

There was nothing he could do but curl up in a ball. He lay like a stone as the morning wore on. A blackbird alighted in the branches above him. Ants crawled over him, but he paid no heed, his eyes open but unseeing. When the sun was near to the middle of the sky, the wind sprang up. Only when he heard a faint, mournful voice did he begin to stir, and then only because the voice echoed what he felt in his broken heart.

The voice grew louder as the wind blew harder, and it faded when the wind abated. Cloud thought it was his own voice crying out the pain in his heart because it was such a hollow, haunted tone rising and floating aimlessly.

Not knowing why, he decided to find who or what the voice belonged to. Scrambling from beneath the cedar branch he stumbled through the grove of trees along a creek.

Something drew him to a particular old, wind-bent cedar as the plaintive voice grew louder. There, halfway up was a dead branch smaller than his wrist. A hollow branch with holes, perhaps drilled by woodpeckers. And with each gust of wind the branch seemed to cry. Cloud had found the voice.

He sat and listened, held fast by the mournful tones that rose and fell with the whim of the wind. At sundown the wind weakened, and so did the voice. Cloud climbed the old cedar and inspected the hollow branch. It was long dead, he could tell, killed by the worms that the woodpeckers were drilling for. In doing so they had opened holes through which the wind flowed and unlocked the strange, mournful voice.

Cloud broke off the branch and climbed down. He sat on the creek bank and blew through the hollow opening, but the voice didn't cry. He noticed that it was like the eagle bone whistle his father had given him and thought it might function much the same.

Placing a small piece of wood over the top hole he was able to coax sound from the hollow branch. At first it was simply noise, but eventually he began to make it sing somewhat like the wind had.

As the sun went down, Cloud paused long enough to gather

dry wood and build a fire. He had no food and his only means of protection was the stone knife in his belt. It did not matter, for his heart was broken. If the great silvertip bear came in the night or some enemy was even now stalking him, he was already dead inside. Dawn Woman was to be the wife of Hollow Horn and bear his children. Life had no meaning.

He kept the fire going far into the night as he sat and blew and blew on the hollow branch. He found that placing his finger-tips over the five holes would lower or raise the pitch. Moreover, when he coaxed the voice from the branch, it strangely eased the pain in his heart. So, of course, he blew and made the branch sing until once again he dropped over from exhaustion.

Morning found him curled next to the cold, gray ashes of his fire pit, his arms around the hollow branch. He awoke lost, un-kempt, and hungry, his heart still torn. Stumbling to the creek, he washed his face and took a long drink and in the water he saw a lonely young man.

He stayed in the grove all day, blowing on the hollow branch. By sundown he could make the branch sing better than the wind had. Through it came the voice of his grief-stricken heart, rising and falling with high and low plaintive notes. Cloud decided that the voice of the branch sounded much like the great cranes that flew overhead each spring and fall. With his knife he carved the end of the branch into the shape of a crane's head and bill. As he made the branch sing, the land and everything on it fell silent listening to the voice of a broken heart.

Another night came, another lonely fire. Another dawn found him next to cold ashes with his pain. Hunger he could push aside, but the only medicine for the pain in his heart was the singing hollow branch. Because he and the wind had given the branch a voice, he decided to call it *hokagapi,* or "to make a voice." It was, of course, a flute.

Another day passed. Cloud blew on his flute and let it cry for him, giving voice to the bottomless pain in his heart. Now and then he paused to work on the flute—reshaping the mouthpiece or making all the finger holes the same size.

He had not eaten for three days. Weak and delirious, he thought he saw Dawn Woman standing by the side of his fire. When he reached out for her, she ran away, or so he thought. So he followed. After a time he simply wandered across the prairie playing the flute, not caring where he was going.

Cloud awoke from a delirious sleep to find himself next to a river. Washing his face and taking a drink, he staggered to the shade of a tree and began blowing on his flute to chase away the pain in his heart. The notes flowed from his flute, rising, falling, and sobbing, crying out the anguish from deep inside. Suddenly, Cloud heard voices and opened his eyes to realize that he was on the riverbank opposite his own village. In his delirium he had found his way home. All the women in the village, young and old, were standing on the other bank staring at him and listening to him play his flute. Among them was Dawn Woman.

The pain of losing her engulfed him like a flash flood. All he could do was blow on the flute and let it cry his anguish. The lilting voice of the flute rose and fell, sighing and sobbing in soft, heartbreaking notes. Cloud noticed that the women were as drawn to the voice of the hollow branch as he had been when he first heard it. There was not a single man in the crowd, only women: old women, young women, and girls all entranced by the crying flute, including Dawn Woman.

Certain that, by now, she was the wife of Hollow Horn, Cloud's grief poured out through his flute. Soon Dawn Woman crossed the river and stood before him, her eyes down but casting frequent bold glances as the flute sang.

"There was a time when a young man I knew made my heart fly," she said softly.

Cloud stopped playing

"Now he sings a strange song that makes my heart sad. What are you doing to me?"

"I am giving my pain a voice," he replied, "because the young woman in my heart has become the wife of another. The spirits have given me this *hokagapi* to do so. I can no longer make her heart fly."

"Can your *hokagapi* sing out in joy?" Dawn Woman asked.

"I can give it no joy, for I do not feel it, and it is I who give this thing its voice."

"But I feel joy at your return," she said. "After you left I knew that life's path without you would be lonely. For, you see, you are in my heart, and always will be. I have taken no husband, unless it would be you."

Cloud could not believe his ears, but he saw the truth in Dawn Woman's eyes. His heart flew and he began playing his flute. This time the flute's song was that of promise, of hope and joy, rising and falling like the wind dancing on the prairies. A song of life.

Once again all the women were enthralled, drawn to the voice of the flute.

The years went by and to the union of Cloud and Dawn Woman were born two sons. As they grew, Cloud taught them to play the flute, and he became known far and wide as the Flutemaker. Young men and boys came to Cloud and asked to learn, and so he taught them all to make and play the flute. And he told them how the spirits had guided him to find the *hokagapi,* taking him from the despair of a broken heart to the joy of a dream fulfilled. That is why, he would tell them, there will always be a hollow tone of sadness in the voice of each flute, to remind everyone that while the flute is played to win love, winning love is also winning the chance of a broken heart. Such is love.

Thereafter on summer evenings, when the fireflies twinkled in the dusk, flutes could be heard singing sweetly, provocatively, up and down the river valleys, their voices touching the heart of any woman, young or old.

Hokagapi, the flute, born of despair, became the voice of courtship, of promise, of hope—and of love.

Man and Woman, Bow and Arrow

I was privileged to witness two eagles performing their court-ship and mating ritual. They began their dance high above the Earth, where they soared and came together in an embrace that locked one to the other. Holding fast to each other they plummeted toward the land. When I thought they would surely crash into the ground, they let go of one another, gained flight and altitude, and then did it all over again. In utter awe and fascination I watched this breathtaking aerial display, realiz-ing suddenly that I was watching life keeping itself in balance while the eagles were fulfilling their purpose and honoring their destiny.

The world works best in balance. To every action there is an opposite and equal reaction, so the scientists say, a dry, unemo-tional premise that suggests a dynamic truth. Up and down, back and forth, night and day, cold and hot, male and female, man and woman: In balance and symmetry is beauty and strength. There are many ways to describe it, to give it an image, but I prefer most the story of the bow and arrow, which was often at the heart of marriage ceremonies in the old days.

A very old man performed the ceremony in those days, and he talked to all the people who gathered. In his hands he would hold a bow and an arrow. He explained that a bow without the arrow is of no use, likewise for the arrow. If a bow is seen alone, one wonders where the arrow is. The same is true of the arrow because one without the other is not balance. But the relation-ship of the bow and arrow is more than togetherness. In order for them to be effective, the arrow must fly true. To do that it must be perfectly straight. Yet no matter how straight the arrow can fly, it can't reach the target unless the bow is strong. One cannot fulfill its purpose without the other.

My grandparents' marriage had been more or less arranged

by my grandmother's mother. After her mother's death my grandmother would inherit a substantial amount of land, and her mother wanted someone to help safeguard her property. My great-grandmother Mollie had always thought highly of my grandfather as a young man. She spoke with his mother, my great-grandmother Elizabeth, and the arrangements were made.

My grandfather was a quiet, hardworking man, a very humble man, and always treated everyone with the utmost respect. I suspect those are the qualities that his future mother-in-law liked. My grandparents were married in 1920, and their marriage lasted until my grandfather died in 1975.

My maternal grandparents raised me. In effect, I was their third child. If they ever raised their voices at each other they didn't do it my presence. They taught me about life not so much by telling me how to live it, but by showing me. I can think of no other couple, except for my paternal grandparents, who treated each other with more respect, respect firmly rooted in unconditional love. I could never think of one without thinking of the other. I couldn't then and I can't now. And when they described the relationship of the bow and arrow, they were talking about themselves.

If there was any weakness that either of them demonstrated, it was the occasional lost look I saw cross my grandmother's face in the years after my grandfather died. I didn't realize how much she missed him until two days before she died. Standing near the foot of her bed in the hospital, I waited for a nurse to leave. A moment or two after the nurse left my grandmother turned her head to the left and spoke. "Do you remember that log house by the river?" she asked quietly, even though there was a tube down her throat. I was about to answer that I didn't remember such a house when I realized she wasn't looking at me. She was looking at a particular spot just to the left of the foot of the bed. There was no one there, at least no one I could see. But no one can tell me that my grandfather wasn't there. No one can convince me that he didn't come for her. No one can tell me he wasn't in the room waiting for her when she died early in the morning two days later.

We laid my grandmother to rest next to my grandfather. As my brothers and I and our male cousins were filling in the grave, I was suddenly compelled to look skyward. There, high above the cemetery, two hawks were soaring together on the wind.

My maternal grandparents' wonderful relationship lasted a lifetime. My paternal grandparents were married fifty-five years before my grandfather Marshall died in 1974. Both couples made a commitment that never wavered and I know without a doubt that they honestly loved one another. Their commitment went beyond this life, as was the case with a neighbor of mine, nearly twenty years ago in a small town on the Rosebud Reservation. She was a middle-aged widow who had lost her husband to a heart attack. Each summer on the anniversary of his death she would rise before dawn and stand on the east side of her house, and as the sun rose she would sing an honoring song for her husband. And throughout the day she would take food to all her neighbors, in his memory. She never remarried. Would that we could all win such love and commitment.

The words to an old Lakota *kahomni,* a round-dance song, express hope and the promise of finding and having love, perhaps of being in balance:

> *My relatives tell me you are asking about me,*
> *We will be together soon.*

Like so many other aspects of our existence—our values, traditions, and customs—love is all about balance. It is the way of the world that in every species there are two life forces: male and female. To deny this reality or walk outside of it would be to create imbalance. To bring a life into this world that is a consequence of lust rather than an offspring of the bond of love between a man and a woman is to give that life a burden that is certainly imbalance. Undeniably, imbalance does occur when someone walks a path outside of the natural order. Even among us, as with every other people the world over, there is homosexuality. But rather than ostracize anyone who treads that path and thereby create further imbalance, we choose tolerance which often promotes understanding over strife. Among us Lakota, as with many other indigenous cultures, we include a place for homosexuals by not denying them the opportunity to be full-fledged members of the community. As such they are a part *of,* and not apart *from;* hence balance is maintained.

The love and hope expressed in the old song is more than the desire for two people to be together. It also carries with it the hope for balance and harmony. In a perfect world two people who truly love one another and are meant for each other are always brought together. But in the real world we know it doesn't always happen, or that it happens in ways we don't always understand. In "The Story of the Cottonwoods" the husband and the wife who eventually stepped aside unselfishly to allow true love to run its course knew that their sacrifice was the right thing to do, no matter how painful it might have been. The union of White Lance and Willow Woman was the world strengthening itself by taking one more step toward balance and harmony. And when they lost their lives prematurely, life itself found a way to reward them for their love and devotion and keep itself in balance.

The young man in "The Story of the Flutemaker" was understandably devastated when the love of his life spurned him. His pain and anguish gave birth to the flute, and it became the voice of his heartbreak. And when he played, the whole world paused to listen because the young man's loss was not his alone. Cloud without Dawn Woman was an imbalance like sunrise without sunset, dark without light, up without down, the bow without the arrow. But when Dawn Woman realized the only course was to follow her heart, balance was restored and thus the flute became an instrument of hope. Each time a flute sings, though it sings of hope and the promise of happiness, there will always be a tone of sadness to remind us there are two sides to everything and the world works best on balance.

As an avid archer I shoot my bows and arrows frequently. My grandfather taught me to handcraft primitive Lakota bows and arrows. A well-made bow and arrow have an aesthetic beauty all their own. There is nothing quite like feeling the power of the bow when it is drawn, unless it is the exhilaration of watching the arrow fly toward its target. This simple activity demonstrates a profound truth: It matters not whether one is the bow or the arrow; what matters is the mutual purpose they fulfill, the balance they achieve.

6

Sacrifice

Icicupi (ee-chee-chu-pee)

To give of oneself, an offering

✛ The Story of the Thunders

In the old days some men took more than one wife. We wonder today what that might be like, to have more than one wife. Sometimes we laugh about it and some of us, deep down, could be a little envious. Back then, however, when a man had more than one wife, it meant that he had to work harder. He had to provide more food, more meat, and more animal hides for clothing. So he had to hunt more. And if more children came, well, then he had to work that much harder. The excitement of having more than one wife was not all there was to it. Most of the time it was for a practical reason, like when a man would take the wife of a friend who was killed in battle. Or he would marry the younger sister of his wife because the first wife wanted it that way. Sometimes things went smoothly; sometimes they did not.

Such was the case with a certain woman in the time before the horses came. The people had moved into the open country. Across what we call the Plains there were many scattered en-campments from the Great Muddy River west as far as the

Black Hills, south to the Running Water River, and north to the Knife River. Some were as close as one or two days of travel and others were many, many days apart.

In one village just east of the Black Hills there was a woman named *Sina Luta,* or Red Shawl. She had married a man who was a good provider and had a good reputation. No children were born to them for many years; then she bore a son. So she was surprised when her husband announced that he would take a second, younger wife. An old man and woman in another village had raised their granddaughter after both her parents had frozen to death in a blizzard. They were getting on in years and wanted to see their granddaughter Necklace married to a good man, so they approached White Wing, Red Shawl's husband, and he had agreed.

Red Shawl never once thought that she would have to share her husband with another woman. Although as first wife—the sits-beside-him wife—she would be able to say how her lodge should be cared for, she was still jealous. When White Wing left to bring home the new wife, Red Shawl packed a few belongings and the bow and arrows he had made for her, and stole away in the night. She tossed scraps of meat to the camp dogs so they wouldn't bark and alert the night sentinels posted around the encampment.

She told no one of her plan, so when her lodge door stayed shut for several days the people suspected she had left but didn't know where she might have gone. Some had seen such things before, a first wife moving out because of jealousy.

Red Shawl traveled east, intending to stay with a cousin who was part of a band living just west of the Great Muddy River. That village meant many, many days of travel, but like all Lakota women of her day, Red Shawl was strong and resourceful. She knew how to hunt, how to be watchful of enemies, and how to pitch a safe, hidden night camp. She could not travel fast because she was carrying her weapons, a large rawhide case filled with food, and her infant son in his cradleboard. He wasn't heavy but he did need to suckle her breast, so she would have to stop often to feed him.

After a few days travel she decided to make camp for a day, mainly to rest her tired feet. Between the sheltering branches of two buffalo-berry thickets high on a slope, she made a cozy camp and spent the day playing with her son. She was still confused over her husband's marriage to a second wife and her heart was broken, but she tried not to think about that.

In the afternoon a warm breeze sang them both to sleep. Toward sundown a deep rumble of thunder woke her, and Red Shawl saw that dark, gray storm clouds had taken away the blue sky. Lightning flashed within the thick, folded clouds and turned the breezes into angry, gusting winds that suddenly bent the buffalo-berry thickets and shook them about. Red Shawl gathered her things and decided to look for better shelter from the rain she knew would come. She remembered a low thicket of chokecherry not far away and hurried toward it.

A summer thunderstorm is the most powerful of the beings that live above the prairie country, second only to the great twisting winds that can uproot great trees and fill the skies with their terrible blackness. Red Shawl had never seen such a wind but was fearful that she might. She had to bend into the gusts to keep from falling and turn away from the wind as leaves stung her face. She covered her baby's cradleboard as small branches flew like arrows and dust stung her eyes.

An angry gust tore her food pack away from her and tossed it a long stone's throw, nearly pulling the cradleboard away, too. She crawled the last few paces to a low thicket, covering her baby with her body to protect him from the wind that was now a steady roar in her ears. Her food gone, her weapons lost, she pushed into the thicket and curled up in a ball with her back to the wind.

Then came wind-driven, heavy, cold drops that felt like pebbles when they hit bare skin, and with them came a sudden darkness. Red Shawl could do nothing but huddle over her baby to shield him from the storm. The rain turned into a cloudburst drenching the land. She was soaked to her skin and her deer hide dress was cold and heavy. Little by little the wind slowed, but the rain kept pounding the land. Tiny streams of water coursed around them and Red Shawl had to lift the cradleboard off the grass to keep her baby as dry as possible. Wiping the water out of her eyes she tried to look around for a high spot, a hill or a knoll, knowing the safest place for them was high ground.

Red Shawl had never been alone in bad weather. In the past, when the winter blizzards soared over the land, she was safe in her mother and father's lodge. When a spring and summer wind storm suddenly fell upon them, everyone in the encampment pounded down the picket pins tight and closed their lodge doors. If there was danger, it didn't seem as bad because many people were around. Now, as the cold rain pelted her face, Red Shawl suddenly understood what it meant to be truly alone. She was alone in a dark land that existed only as far as she could see.

She hung on tight to the cradleboard and headed for the south side of a long gully, hoping to climb its ridge and find some shelter, any shelter. Slipping and sliding in the mud slowed her down, so she stopped to rest in the lee side of a sturdy cottonwood tree. The rain kept coming down heavier and heavier until every low area was running with water. A soft whimper reminded her that her breasts were full and it was time to feed the baby. Turning away from the rain as much as she could, she opened the covering of the cradleboard and fed the hungry baby. For a few moments she forgot about the rain as she enjoyed the closeness she felt with her baby. He was so hungry he quickly drained her breast so she switched him to the other.

Resting against the tree, Red Shawl shivered in her wet clothes, thankful that she had managed to keep the baby as dry as possible. The sudden storm had shaken her up, reminding her that life was a journey full of the unexpected, like a second wife for her husband. She knew his reason for taking that sec-

ond wife was not to replace her but to provide a place for someone who would need a provider and protector.

Red Shawl looked at her son, at his trusting eyes. Her fit of
girlish jealousy had placed him in danger. She felt small and
foolish. When the storm passed, she would head home, she decided. The wind had taken away her food and weapons and it
would be beyond foolish to continue her journey. Perhaps, she
thought, the wind was trying to teach her a lesson. Red Shawl
drew her son close and then heard a low, rumbling noise.

A strange kind of thunder seemed to roll down from the sky.
Then she realized it was not thunder from the clouds or the
wind. It was a flash flood rolling down a deep gully, the gully she
was in.

Red Shawl had never in her life seen anything like the mass of
dark, rolling water rushing toward her. Broken tree branches
rolled with the churning water, reaching up and out like hands
wanting to pull her in. It was no use to run, she knew, the rolling
water would sweep them away. She forced herself to look away
from the approaching death and somehow looked up to the fork
of the sturdy cottonwood. But there was no time to climb.

She stood and reached up as high as she could and jammed
the cradleboard into the fork of the tree. Tying the straps around
the fork, she prayed even as she wept. "Grandfather, take me if
you must, but spare my son!" The cold water grabbed her legs
and pulled her into its churning black current.

Red Shawl awoke in cold and blackness, yet her body seemed
hot with pain as she coughed and coughed. After painfully
pulling herself to a sitting position, she realized she was caught
in sandbar willows. She was somewhere near a river or a creek,
she thought, because sandbar willows only grew along stream
banks. Then she heard the gurgling voice of flowing water. Remembering the flood, she tried to jump to her feet. A hot, stab-
bing pain in her ankle stopped her and she had to lean back
until the pain passed. In the blackness of the night sky above
she saw stars. The storm had passed.

Shivering, she tried to remember everything, but the only picture in her mind was a churning wall of dark, murky water. Except for the cold night air, the pain in her ankle, and the fullness in her breasts, she was without feeling or memories. Then her heart seemed to stop. Her breasts were full, ready to be suckled. Her baby! Where was her baby?

Memories of the day past swept her away, throwing her down into a dark hole of despair. She had lived through the flash flood, but she had lost her baby. Red Shawl curled up in the cold, wet mud and wept. The pain in her ankle was nothing compared to the searing grief in her heart. She tore at her hair and clothes as her pain cried out from the pit of her being, then she pounded the mud until her fists were numb.

Slowly, then, a clear memory of the flood began to push itself into her mind, like the sun chasing away a storm cloud. Red Shawl remembered the sturdy cottonwood tree; she remembered putting the cradleboard in the fork and tying it fast. She wept again, but this time in hope. Perhaps the flood hadn't taken her baby. Perhaps the cottonwood had been strong enough to stand in the churning current. Ignoring the pain in her ankle, she rose and staggered around in the darkness. There was only one thing to do: Find that tree.

Though the sky was filled with stars there was no moon. As her mind began to clear she could hear coyotes barking all around her, then wolves howling far away. There were other things in the darkness that were far more dangerous than coyotes or wolves: Bears were known to maim and kill two-leggeds. Likewise the great cat. All the more reason to find her baby.

Red Shawl heard the birds beginning to awaken, then noticed a pale glow over a horizon. Dawn was approaching. That meant she had been knocked out for most of the night, and she wondered how far the flood had carried her. Slowly, slowly the light grew and shadows took the shapes of hills and trees. Waiting was difficult, but she knew it would be wiser to be patient until there was more light.

She was glad to know which way was east. Light gave her a chance to look at her injured ankle. It was badly sprained, though she couldn't remember how. Somewhere in the hazy distance she heard the bellow of a bull buffalo and the trilling call of a redwing blackbird's morning song. Life started new each day and Red Shawl prayed that her baby was somewhere alive.

Hawks took to the sky and soared on the cool morning breezes. A river was close because the valley was full of trees and the mist from its waters hung above them, but she couldn't recognize the land. She was far from home, though like all Lakota she was a good traveler, always looking at her back trail—something she had been taught as a girl. She would have recognized country she had passed through. Immediately she looked around for the slope with the sturdy cottonwood, hoping that she had not been swept far from that, but she could see nothing familiar.

As the first rays of the new sun hit her face, she stood and turned west. There were some realities in her favor. The storm had come from the west and the cottonwood tree in which she had put her baby had been on the east-facing slope. The flood had come from the west and had swept her down slope to the east, toward the river. Behind her the river was flowing north. She could have been swept into it somewhere to the south, to her left, and carried along by its flood-swollen current to where she had awakened. Rethinking all of this, she turned her limping steps to the south.

Red Shawl ignored the hunger in her stomach. A gentle morning breeze chilled her but helped to dry out her dress. She was barefoot and bare-legged, her moccasins and leggings taken by the flood. Grabbing a broken branch, she used it as a walking stick. She kept a steady pace knowing she couldn't walk fast with her injured ankle. At midmorning she stopped at a cool spring and drank its clear water. The day was warming and it gave her renewed hope. Close to midday she paused to rest her ankle and realized she had reached the gully that had been flooded. Great piles of broken branches and flattened grass silently told the story of yesterday's flash flood.

She gasped as she recognized the sturdy cottonwood. Ignoring her throbbing ankle she tried to run, but even as she drew near to the tree she saw that its branches held no cradleboard. Perhaps, she tried to reason, this isn't the tree. But the torn-up gully could not be mistaken. She reached the tree and knew she had been here; she knew that she had placed her son in the right fork and tied his cradleboard to it. There was nothing here.

Red Shawl fell to the ground and wept. If only she had stayed home. If only she had not gotten angry over her husband's second wife. Wiping away her tears, she stood and followed the path of the flood, looking for the cradleboard with her son in it. The path of destruction was easy to follow. She had been swept along here and she wondered how it was that she was still alive. At the river's edge she turned and followed it north. When the sun was low in the western sky, she had returned to the spot she had awakened. She had not eaten and had taken water only once, but she didn't care. She wanted to die.

Like the day before, clouds rimmed over the western horizon. But this day they were white and billowy, not low and dark. Resting against a small oak, Red Shawl wept quietly. "You who live in the clouds," she prayed, "take pity on my son; he is so small and helpless. Take his spirit up to Grandfather. And if you would be so kind, I want to be with my son."

Red Shawl cried herself to sleep. She awoke just after sundown to a strange feeling in her full breasts, reminding her of her mind-numbing loss. Night was coming as she wept again, great sobs shaking her body. Mercifully, the weariness of her body, weak from hunger, dragged her into sleep.

A frightening dream of dark, swirling water woke her sometime in the night. To the west was a distant rumble of thunder and flashes of lightening. She immediately recalled her situation and fell into despair knowing that she had failed as a mother and a wife. "You who live in the clouds," she prayed once again as thunder rolled beyond the horizon. "Be kind to my son. Take him where it is safe."

She thought that she would never be remembered as a good woman but as a foolish and jealous one who caused the death of her own son. In her mind she could see him, his dark eyes looking up at her with trust. It was all that she would ever have of him.

The honorable thing to do was go back to the village, she thought, and tell White Wing that her foolishness had killed their son. Even if he were to forgive her, she could never forgive herself. Though he was a good man, Red Shawl knew it was not likely that White Wing would welcome her back. It would be more likely that she would be banished from the village and forced to wander alone for the rest of her life.

Once more the soft, round little face of her son appeared in her mind. She could hear his soft voice, too. Perhaps that's what grief did to someone, she thought, as she wept quietly. When she finally calmed herself, she heard the soft voice again. In her despair she reached out, and touched something in the darkness. Lightning flashed and in that instant of light she saw the cradleboard, and heard her son cry out in hunger.

Disbelief tormented her. She expected the image of her son to fade away in the next heartbeat. But it didn't. Instead he cried out again. With a shout of joy she grabbed the cradleboard and breathed on his tiny face. He was there!

Red Shawl's joy knew no bounds. "Thank you, Grandfather!" she cried. "Thank you, you who live in the clouds!"

She unwrapped him from the cradleboard and fed him. He eagerly suckled her breasts, filling what seemed his bottomless hunger. Then she took him into the water and they bathed together. They slept on a grassy slope, caressed by a warm breeze. In the light of a new day they began their journey home.

Sometime on the second day White Wing appeared and Red Shawl was overjoyed yet again. From their appearance he could tell that his wife and son had been through a difficult time. He made camp and saw to their comfort.

"I have decided to take Necklace back to her grandparents," he said. "There are many good men who could take her for a wife."

"No," said Red Shawl, "that would bring her shame. I will welcome her into our lodge because I will always be honored to be your first wife." Then she told him about the flood, and that their son had been lost and then returned by the Thunders.

Though she never questioned why her son had been returned, for the rest of her life Red Shawl wondered how it had happened. It was a joyful mystery and a reality that was sometimes hard to believe, one that she looked upon as a gift. To show gratitude for such a gift she knew she had to give of herself in return, so Red Shawl took her rightful place as White Wing's first wife and welcomed Necklace as she would a sister. In time they became close, and both were known far and wide as selfless and devoted mothers.

Red Shawl's son grew tall and strong and was devoted to his mother. When he was fifteen, White Wing bestowed on the boy the name his mother had given him. For the rest of his life he was known as *Wakinyan Aglipi*, Brought Back by the Thunders.

Red Shawl lived a long life and was regarded by many as a good, wise woman. When someone would praise her for her wisdom, she would thank them and quietly tell the story of how her son came by his name. And how even foolishness can lead to wisdom.

Those who knew her would listen in the spring and summer, especially when the thunders rumbled and lightning flashed inside the great rolling clouds. They would listen as she stood outside her lodge singing an honor song for those who lived in the clouds.

The Gift of Self

A creation story describes our people coming up into the world through a hole in the Earth. One person remained behind. Those who came out liked this place of light and warmth and decided to stay. It was obviously the right decision because the people wanted for nothing. Everyone was happy until hard times came. Drought laid waste to the land and famine came thereafter; the people became weak and began to die. The one who had stayed behind saw what was happening to those who had left and was sad to see them suffering. That last one came out of the hole and became the bison, the *tatanka,* and multiplied until they covered the Earth. The people hunted the bison and ate its flesh and were saved. As time went on, the people saw other ways to use the bison; from its hide they made coverings for their dwellings, from its bones they made toys and weapons, from its hair they made rope, and from its horns they made spoons and cups. Every part of the bison was put to use. The people became strong again; in fact, they grew stronger than they were before. For that they honored the sacrifice of the bison in their songs and dances.

In June of 1876, eight days before the Battle of the Little Bighorn, somewhere between seven hundred to nine hundred Lakota and Sahiyela (Northern Cheyenne) warriors led by Crazy Horse met General George Crook's thirteen-hundred-man column at Rosebud Creek, some fifty miles south of the Little Bighorn, and fought them to a standstill in a day-long battle. During the fighting, a prominent Sahiyela war leader was unhorsed within mere yards of the enemy's position. As he sought to escape on foot, a rider broke from the Sahiyela ranks, rode through intense enemy gunfire, and rescued the Sahiyela leader. The rider was a woman named Buffalo Calf Road, and she risked her life to rescue her brother.

Eleven months after the Lakota victory at the Battle of the Little Bighorn, the Oglala Lakota leader Crazy Horse made a fateful decision. He decided to surrender to the United States government. Of his 900 followers, less than 130 were fighting men. The rest were the elderly, and women, and children. It was for the best interests of the latter group that Crazy Horse made his decision. The army had intensified its campaign against the Lakota after the humiliating defeat at the Little Bighorn, and Crazy Horse's biggest problem was one of numbers. His fighting men were badly outnumbered by the soldiers. The loss of even one Lakota fighting man meant a significant loss of protection for noncombatants, not to mention that a family would lose a father or a son. Unlike the Americans, the Lakota (and other Plains tribes) did not have a standing army apart from the rest of the community. There were times when groups of fighting men, popularly called war parties, took to the field for patrol and reconnaissance duties for days and sometimes weeks, but they always returned to the encampment or village where their families were. Noncombatants were rarely left totally unprotected; therefore, the males of fighting age did more than fight. Most of them were also husbands, fathers, hunters, horse trainers, teachers, and so on.

In his military persona the average Lakota fighting man, the warrior, was a formidable guerilla fighter, and man for man he was better trained for fighting than the average cavalry or infantry soldier. For those reasons there was talk among the Crazy Horse warriors of hiding their noncombatants and taking to the field as the highly mobile, superb cavalry they were. But the logistical problem of finding a safe hiding place for the elderly and the women and children, and ensuring that they had adequate provisions, could not be solved. Even if that were possible, the older, more experienced warriors were certain that the army would find the helpless ones and attack them once they knew they had no effective protection. Their propensity for doing that was well known. General William Harney had attacked a

Sicangu Laktoa camp in 1855 while most of the men were away hunting. Harney's soldiers killed women and children, and he was thereafter dubbed Woman Killer by the Sicangu. In 1868 the Seventh Cavalry attacked a peaceful Cheyenne village at the Washita River in Kansas, and most of the casualties were women and children. And, of course, the bitterest memory of all was Chivington's massacre of Cheyenne women and children at Sand Creek, Colorado, in 1864. As a fifteen-year-old boy, Crazy Horse had seen the aftermath of the Harney attack, and that was the basis for his lifelong mistrust of the whites.

Crazy Horse and others could see what lay ahead. Further resistance meant certain death for everyone because the whites were much too numerous. Indeed, he didn't know how right he was. In the late 1870s the total population of all the Plains tribes, about 40 tribes from south to north, was probably between 250,000 to 300,000. The population of the United States was 25 million. The Lakota had dwindled to less than 15,000, and most of them were already on reservations.

So the decision was made to surrender, and nine hundred people sacrificed their freedom for an uncertain future. Crazy Horse already knew all about such sacrifices. His Sicangu Lakota uncle, Spotted Tail, a formidable warrior in his own right and a leader among the Sicangu as a young man, had surrendered himself to the soldiers in 1855. He took another man's place to be punished for an offense against the whites he didn't commit. Spotted Tail and a few other Sicangu men, along with their families, were taken to Fort Leavenworth, Kansas, to be imprisoned. Spotted Tail's relatives mourned for him because none of the Lakota who had been taken to Fort Leavenworth before had ever returned. But Spotted Tail did return and with a newfound respect for the whites, not because they were a good people but because there were too many of them—the same lesson Crazy Horse learned twenty-two years later.

Life demands much from us. We are all called upon to make sacrifices for ourselves and more often for others. And sacrifice comes in many forms. Cemeteries all over the world are full of people who have made the ultimate sacrifice in the name of duty, patriotism, or ideology. We'll never know how many fighting men from all of the Indian tribes died trying to protect their homelands and their way of life against white invasion.

Wars and other cataclysmic events will always give rise to heroes, but life, thankfully, is quite ordinary for many of us. We may not wake up to a war in our residential neighborhood or find ourselves caught up in social or political upheaval, but some measure of sacrifice is often necessary nonetheless, such as parents working two jobs to enable their children's dreams, whether it's a college education or a pair of Nikes for basketball. The list is endless and most parents put forth their efforts without complaint. These acts or deeds of sacrifice are the gift of self.

The gift of self is the most meaningful anyone can give. A rich man who writes a check to a hospital to build a new research facility is certainly an epitome of generosity. Generosity is a necessary virtue, but unless that man has given away all of his money he has not performed an act of sacrifice.

A man had a wife and a daughter. He worked long and hard at his job and never failed to give them all they wanted and needed materially. The girl's room was full of expensive toys, and she wore the latest fashionable clothes. One evening he happened to visit his daughter in her room and was puzzled to see the array of expensive toys languishing at the back of the room. Next to the girl's bed, at eye level, was a scrap of paper—a handwritten note—pinned to the wall. The man recognized his own handwriting. It was a note he had hurriedly written because he couldn't attend her birthday party. It read, "My apologies. Love, Dad." The expensive gift of jewelry he had left with the note was nowhere to be seen. "Why," he asked his daughter, "is this worthless piece of paper hanging on the wall?" "Because," his daughter replied, "it's the only thing I have that is really from you."

The most sacred of Lakota spiritual practices is the *Wi-wanyang Wacipi,* or the "looking at the sun and dancing," more popularly known as the Sun Dance. For non-Indians it is probably the most intriguing and the most misunderstood. Most non-Indians are appalled or turned off by what they describe as "self-torture," the skin-piercing that some participants must endure. The piercing is done to male dancers who have pledged to perform the dance. The skin of the upper chest, the pectoral region, is pierced in two places and skewers made of bone are inserted. To the skewers is attached a cord that is tied to a central pole. The participants pull the cord tight as they dance, the object being to tear the skewers through their flesh. Other participants may be skewered through the skin on their backs, and they pull several buffalo skulls as they dance.

The United States government, at the urging of many Christian churches that characterized the dance as uncivilized and barbaric, outlawed the Sun Dance. They failed or chose not to see the ceremony for what it was: a symbolic act of sacrifice.

The Sun Dance is still with us because it demonstrates to us that sacrifice must be a genuine and operative virtue in our culture. The Sun Dancer gives of himself in spite of the terrible pain of being pierced and having skewers tear through his flesh. One obviously doesn't endure such pain for frivolous reasons. Participation may be an act of thanksgiving, for example, but it is always real and symbolic and reminds us that sacrifice—no matter how painful—is often necessary. To perform the Sun Dance is to truly give or offer the one gift that is most meaningful: the gift of self, which is all any of us truly has to give.

I can recall my grandmother doing laundry for my uncle when he was in college. She would be the first to say that it was all part of her job. My uncle was at the University of South Dakota some 250 miles away. He sent his laundry home by parcel post in a suitcase; Grandma would wash it by hand in a galvanized tub with a washboard, hang everything up to dry on the outdoor line, and then do the ironing. If the wind and the sun cooperated, it was a day's chore. I can remember her ironing those white shirts by lamplight late at night. She would meticulously fold them and repack them in the suitcase, which then meant that Grandpa and I would haul the suitcase, by a team and wagon, to the rural mailbox on the highway. As I recall, this happened on a regular biweekly schedule. I know, without a doubt, that my uncle appreciated those efforts because there weren't many laundromats on campus in those days. Sending the laundry home proved to be a labor-intensive process because we had no electricity in the late 1940s. Water had to be heated on the wood stove, the laundry hung on an outdoor line and then taken down, and the heavy iron heated on the stove. I'll always have this point of reference for the phrase "doing the laundry."

My grandparents made plenty of sacrifices for me as well. For reasons that still are not clear to me, I must have changed schools at least a dozen times before I graduated from high school. My grandparents moved to be near me a few times. More than a few times my grandmother did my laundry, sewed on buttons, darned socks, and so on. I appreciated those chores she did, but I know she thought of them as nothing more than little labors of love within the job description of a grandmother. There were hundreds of those little chores, perhaps thousands, that she performed for me and my siblings. I still appreciate them, not because of a patch on a pair of trousers or a freshly ironed shirt, but because of the lesson that came with them. She taught me how to give of myself.

Sacrifices come in all sizes and for every reason under the sun, and there are times when we can be unaware that someone has made one for us or because of us. Tough and extraordinary circumstances will always bring extraordinary individuals to the top with their acts of selfless courage and sacrifice. History has its Crazy Horses, Spotted Tails, and Buffalo Calf Roads. We will never forget their deeds or their sacrifices. Ordinary, everyday people also make sacrifices and remind us that it is within human nature to do so. We stand and offer our seats on the bus or the subway, or we step back to let someone ahead of us in line. We help the elderly travelers near us in line carry their bags to the ticket counter. A mom does without new clothes so she can buy them for her children. A man checks on his vacationing neighbor's house, and waters and mows the lawn. These are simple acts, but they can give us all a sense of dignity and an example to follow.

My cousin Israel Knife and I were deer hunting near the confluence of the Little and Big White Rivers in the fall of 1964. Israel was extremely shy around white folks. In fact, he would always ask me to order for him in restaurants. But by ourselves in the back country, or anywhere white folks weren't around, he could talk my ear off.

We didn't have much luck on this particular day, so we wearily trudged back to a trail where our ride, Israel's dad, would pick us up. Just west of the Little White River we heard a commotion in some trees, a veritable tirade of cussing and shouting. Soon we found the source of the noise: two out-of-state white hunters who had somehow managed to entangle the antlers of a five-point white-tailed buck in the strands of an unyielding three-strand barbed-wire fence. With the antlers caught, the dead deer wasn't going anywhere, no matter how the two hunters tried to disentangle it. In fact, they did nothing but exacerbate the situation—they were twisting the antlers tighter into the wire. Having exhausted all alternatives, from their point of view, the hunters' next recourse was to cut off the head and leave it caught in the fence. As they each whipped out a Bowie knife with a twelve-inch blade, I suggested that a game warden might take a dim view of a headless deer carcass.

Israel and I studied the puzzle of the tangled antlers. We inserted sturdy twigs at a few strategic places, untwisted the wire, and freed the antlers. The deer fell to the ground, and I swear he looked quite relieved. Then we carefully dragged the carcass under the bottom strand and turned it over to the two astonished hunters.

"How did you do that?" asked one.

"Why did you do that?" asked the other.

"Somebody had to," replied Israel. It was the first time I ever heard him use a disgusted, and at the same time, amused tone of voice to a white man.

They offered us money, which we declined. We walked away, and when we turned to look back, they were still staring at us, their jaws hanging open.

"Money would have been nice," I said.

"Yes," replied Israel, "but just think. Every time those two go deer hunting or see a deer, they're going to think about two Indian boys."

Amazing what the gift of self can do.

7

Truth

Wowicake (wo-wee-jah-keh)

That which is real, the way the world is

The Story of the Trickster's Song

Iktomi's stomach was growling as he crawled out of the deserted bear's den where he had been sleeping. He woke up hungry, but that was nothing new to Iktomi. He liked to sleep more than anything, so he was hungry a lot. Still, he wasn't too worried. He always found a way to feed himself, though it wasn't because he was a good hunter. Iktomi was not a hunter at all. His only real skill was that he was tricky, one of the trickiest beings around. He preferred living off the work or the mistakes of others. At that he was very good. That was the truth about Iktomi.

He rubbed sleep from his eyes and looked around. It was a fine summer afternoon. The cottonwood tree's leaves were singing in the playful breeze while the grasses danced. Redwing blackbirds added their bright call, and somewhere a meadowlark joined in. Not far away, in the shade of an oak grove, white-tailed deer dozed in the cool shade of a plum thicket.

Iktomi didn't care about such things unless they somehow meant he could be more comfortable. He didn't see anything that meant he could eat, so he set out across the prairie to look for a quick meal. The chokecherries, plums, and buffalo-berries were not yet ripe, and he hadn't forgotten his stomachache from eating green berries, so he ignored them. There were fish—bullheads—in the river, but that meant he would have to catch grasshoppers for bait. He wouldn't eat fish today because grasshoppers were much too fast, too hard to catch.

He rested on a hilltop after a long climb. As he sat looking out over the rolling prairies, he thought he heard laughter on the wind. Sweaty and hungry, his mood was like a blustery, black cloud, and laughter was the last thing he wanted to hear. Still, he was curious and listened closely. There it was: laughter from many voices, like the sound of an annoying mosquito.

Curiosity pushed aside his annoyance. Anything unusual was always good to look into, since it could mean food. Iktomi listened and started walking in the direction of the laughter. The trouble was that the prairie has low, rolling hills in every direction, and the wind can play tricks. Sometimes the laughter seemed to come from behind him and sometimes from the left or right. After stumbling to the top of several hills, Iktomi noticed that the noise was louder, and with the laughter he heard splashing. He knew there was a small, shallow lake nearby and decided to look there.

Iktomi grinned after he came to the top of yet another hill. Opportunity seemed to be favoring him this day. There was the lake, and on it was a large flock of ducks. They were laughing and dancing on the water, splashing and having a good time. And they were so busy having fun they didn't see Iktomi. His stomach growled louder.

He hid behind a soapweed and began thinking of a plan. Iktomi was always at his best when he was driven by hunger, so thoughts flashed in his mind like lightning. With a self-satisfied smile he sneaked down to a creek bottom and quickly gathered a large bundle of sticks. Tying them together snugly, he hoisted the bundle onto his back and set out for the lake, and the ducks.

From the top of the hill he walked purposefully down, the

bundle of wood on his back, and he bent beneath it as if it were a heavy load. He keep his eyes straight ahead and never once looked in the direction of the singing and dancing ducks.

As he knew would happen, one of the ducks spotted Iktomi and shouted a warning. "Look out! It's Iktomi!" He was well known to the ducks, for he would eat anything. Some of the ducks took to wing, and a hush fell over the lake. Strangely, Iktomi took no notice of the anxious flock. He continued on, bent under his load of wood, seemingly in a hurry.

The ducks who had fled returned to the lake. They all watched the strange sight of Iktomi bent under a bundle of wood, marching purposefully onward and ignoring them. No one, no matter who, likes to be ignored. And Iktomi was ignoring the ducks, not for a moment acknowledging that they were in the same world. He kept walking; his stomach kept growling. Soon he was past them and walking away from the lake. It was more than they could stand.

"Iktomi!" one of them called out.

Iktomi kept walking.

"Iktomi!" they called out with one voice.

Iktomi paused, his eyes blinking vaguely as he glanced about. He slowly turned toward the lake and saw the ducks. Surprise registered on his face.

"Hau," he called out. "My friends, are you well? What are you doing?"

"We are dancing, celebrating," they told him. "It's such a good day!"

"I am happy for you!" Iktomi called back. Then looking off, he turned to leave.

The ducks didn't know what to do, nor how to act. Iktomi was not acting like Iktomi. It was too much for them. They had to know why.

"Wait!" they called. "What are you doing? Why are you carrying all that wood?"

Iktomi wiped his brow and seemed anxious to go. "This is

not wood, you see," he told them. "These are songs. For sure they are sacred songs. I'm taking them to a celebration over there by the river." He shifted his load and started walking. "They are waiting for me; I have to get there before sunset."

The ducks raised a commotion, all of them shouting. "Wait! Wait! Don't go yet, sing us one of the songs so we can dance!"

Iktomi hesitated, thinking deeply for a moment. "No, I can't," he replied, "I have a long way to go and they're waiting. Besides, these are sacred songs and I don't think I should sing one to you people. I don't know you."

"Don't go!" they shouted. "We want to hear one of those songs!"

Iktomi sighed and stopped, waving his hands impatiently. "I do need to rest," he said, sitting down in the grass as his stomach rumbled again. "I've been walking since sunrise. After I catch my breath, perhaps I can sing you one song. But I don't know . . . these are sacred songs and I don't know if you should hear them."

The ducks raised a clamor. "No, No! We want to hear a song! Just one!" They all swam to the shore, waddled onto the grass, and surrounded Iktomi, their little beady eyes pleading with him. It was very hard for Iktomi not to reach out and snatch one because they were all fat, and he knew the meat would be tender and juicy roasted over the fire. His stomach growled and he laughed to cover the noise as he sighed and wiped his brow. "Yes, yes," he muttered. "I'll sing you one song, then I must be on my way."

Quacking joyously, the ducks clamored back into the water, laughing in anticipation. It wasn't often they could dance to a sacred song. Iktomi nearly drooled as he watched them, but he knew he had to play out the ruse or he would go hungry again.

After a moment he carefully untied his bundle and laid out the sticks and studied each one. He would pick up a stick, mumble and hum, shake his head, then put it down and pick up another. The ducks, of course, were curious.

"What are you doing?" they asked.

"I'm looking for the right song for you. I must find the one that will be good for you," he explained wisely.

"Yes," said the ducks, "pick out the right one. We will wait."

Iktomi dutifully picked up one stick after another, mumbling and humming, until he found the one he wanted. It was a sturdy stick, of course, and was just right for what he had in mind. To the ducks it was the right song.

"This is the one!" he announced. The ducks cheered; their quacking was loud and annoying, but Iktomi smiled.

"Now," he said, "since this is a sacred song, there is something you must do when I start singing."

"Tell us," the ducks yelled, "tell us what to do!"

"When I begin to sing, you must close your eyes tightly. This is a sacred song and it has powers. I don't know what will happen if you open your eyes. I will close my eyes, too, because I know how powerful these songs are. They are so powerful that I was told never to sing them with my eyes open, and others who hear them must also close their eyes. Do you understand?"

"Yes! Yes! We understand," they clamored.

Iktomi found a soft, grassy spot and sat, holding the stick. He cleared his throat. "I must warn you," he said, "if you open your eyes while I'm singing, your eyes will turn red and stay that way. So no matter what happens, no matter what you hear, keep your eyes closed. This is a sacred song, and who knows what powers will come when I sing?"

"We will keep our eyes closed," they promised.

Iktomi cleared his throat, closed his eyes, and bowed his head for a long moment. Then he began to sign. *"Heya hey hey hey heya ha . . ."* His voice rose and fell rhythmically, for if nothing else Iktomi was a good singer. Perhaps that went along with being tricky.

The ducks were impressed with Iktomi's fine singing voice. They closed their eyes and swam out and began to dance.

Iktomi poured his heart into the song because of his stomach, of course. It was empty and growling. The ducks splashed and swayed to the song, their eyes tightly shut. Iktomi opened one eye slightly. The water was white with the splashing the ducks made. His mouth watered at the sight of so much food, but he kept singing, louder and louder.

When he was certain the ducks were totally engrossed in the dance, Iktomi rose to his feet and walked along the shore, first one way and then the other. He began to dance, too, so that if one of the ducks happened to open his eyes, he would see that Iktomi was dancing with them. But not one did.

After several passes back and forth along the shore, so that his voice came from several directions, Iktomi waded carefully into the water. Slowly, slowly he worked his way toward the ducks as they continued to dance and splash. Then Iktomi hefted his stick, testing its balance as he took a few practice swings, singing all the time, of course.

Finally he was in among the ducks as their fat, succulent bodies bobbed on the water in time to Iktomi's song. He danced, making loud splashing noises himself. The ducks kept on dancing, unaware of the slobbering, hungry grin on Iktomi's face.

With a swift, skillful swing Iktomi bashed one of the ducks, but there was so much splashing the others took no notice. Encouraged, he swung again. A little while later he swung the club again, and again. Soon seven ducks were floating dead in the water while the others continued splashing and dancing. Iktomi could already imagine the ducks roasting over a fire, and his hunger rose like a hot wind.

Throwing caution aside Iktomi flailed away, still singing. Several more ducks fell victim to his club until there was not as much splashing. A duck opened his eyes and saw Iktomi among them and several of his fellows floating lifeless on the water.

"Look out!" the duck cried. "Fly away, fly away, or Iktomi will kill us all!"

Other ducks opened their eyes to see the carnage and in a

whir of wings they fled from the hungry Iktomi. But for many of them it was too late.

Iktomi's song turned into a gleeful laugh as he began to gather his booty. The remaining ducks were long over the horizon, out of his reach. But to a duck their eyes had turned red because they opened their eyes during Iktomi's song. To this day their descendants have red eyes, also. They can be seen, now and then, flying above or floating on a pond, cautiously throwing red-eyed glances right and left, always on the lookout for Iktomi.

Iktomi feasted until he could eat no more, roasting ducks over the flames from the bundle of wood he had gathered as his sacred songs. Then he found a place to sleep.

So if Iktomi comes and says he has songs for you, don't close your eyes when he sings. The trouble is, who knows what form Iktomi might take when he comes to you?

Seeing the Way Things Are

An Easterner moved to the West to live the slow-paced, elemental lifestyle he had always yearned after. In the autumn he purchased a rustic log house at the base of a mountain. Since his only source of heat was a wood stove, he set about laying in wood. Soon he had a very large pile of wood next to his house. But since his only preparation for winter previously had been to turn up the thermostat in his apartment, he didn't know if he had put up enough wood to keep him warm through the winter. So he decided to ask a few local people.

"Go to the top of the mountain," a neighbor advised. "Up there lives a wise old Indian. He can give you the advice you need."

So the Easterner climbed the mountain, which was no simple task for someone used to stairs and escalators, and found an old

Indian man sitting in front of a tiny log cabin. "I was wondering," he said, getting immediately to the point, "I have a wood stove to heat my house. How will I know how much wood is enough to last the winter through?"

The old Indian stood, walked to the edge of the mountain, looked up into the sky, into the surrounding forest, and down the mountain, and returned to his chair. "More wood," he uttered.

The Easterner climbed back down and went to work, and in a week or so he had a pile of wood half the size of his house. He felt better, but soon the doubts began to creep in, so he decided to visit the old Indian once again. The climb to the top of the mountain was no easier the second time, but the old Indian was there still. "I've put up more wood, but I'm still not sure I have enough," he confessed.

Whereupon the old Indian stood, walked to the edge of the mountain, looked up into the sky, into the surrounding forest, and down the mountain, and returned to his chair. "More wood," he uttered.

The Easterner climbed back down and went back to work. In two weeks he doubled his wood pile and was feeling more secure, certain now that he would stay warm through the entire winter. But he was curious about how that old Indian on the mountain knew how much wood was enough. So he decided to ask him.

After yet another long, arduous climb the Easterner found the old Indian sitting in front of his log cabin. "Sir," he said, "I have more than enough wood to last me through the winter. I thank you for your advice, but I must know the basis of your wisdom. I noticed you looked up into the sky and into the forest. Is that how you knew how much wood I would need to get me through the winter?"

"Not really," replied the old Indian. "Below me lives a white man and he's been laying in the wood like you wouldn't believe. That's how I knew."

⟡⟡⟡

I asked my grandfather once, when he was in his sixties, I believe, if he could tell me what truth was. "I don't think I've lived
long enough to know that," he said, "all I know is that without
it Iktomi would be the most powerful being on Earth. And
that's the truth."

Having lived more than half a century, I think I'm just beginning to gain some insight into my grandfather's reply. Truth is
often difficult to distinguish. It can be a gift or a burden; it can
be kind or cruel. It frequently eludes our grasp and we find it
difficult to describe. Truth can at times hide so well that we
can't find it to save ourselves, or it disguises itself so skillfully
that we walk all over it without knowing. And in the next instance it becomes plain as day, whether we want it to or not. In
the end we learn we can't live without it.

"Truth is the marker along the roads we travel in life," my
grandfather did say. The Red Road has many markers. If you
choose the Black Road, there is only the illusion of truth. We
can be influenced by truth or by illusion.

Two chieftains met on a plain while their two armies waited.
"I have ten thousand warriors, every one skilled with weapons
and seasoned by battle. Victory will be mine," said the first
chieftain. "What do you have?"

"Only the truth," replied the second chieftain. "This war
has decimated my people so I face you now with an army of a
thousand children. This truth will either destroy you or glorify
you."

The first chieftain returned to his camp, where his army of
ten thousand stood ready for battle. He ordered his army to put
aside their weapons while he went into seclusion to ponder the
truth his enemy had spoken. With the new dawn he sent his
chief aide with gifts of food and an offer of peace to the army of
a thousand children. The first chieftain then returned to his
homeland and stood to be judged before his countrymen, fully

expecting to be dishonored for his weakness. He was, instead, made a king.

Sometimes truth is like the wind. You can't see it, but you can see the effect it has. Truth is also like sunrise and sunset. We see the sun come up over the eastern horizon in the morning and then disappear behind the western horizon in the evening. From the perspective of our existence on a spinning sphere, the sun appears to "rise" and "set." In reality the sun does neither.

Reality is what is, first and foremost, in our physical world. In the Lakota world reality is, for example, that the four seasons cycle in precisely the same order year after year. Reality is that lakes and rivers freeze in winter and thaw in the spring, that all living things die, that change is inevitable.

Truth is the result of the trials and errors of life, the lessons we have learned such as "Without evil, goodness would be harder to recognize," or "The first casualty of war is truth," or "A bird in the hand is worth two in the bush." Some rise out of the illusions we have acquired: for example, "Good will always prevail over evil." Truth is subjective, as in the story of the blind men and the elephant. It is also subject to change, as in "Man was not intended to fly."

If there is a universal human weakness, it is that we want to believe there is truth because we want clear answers rather than illusions, and therefore we are vulnerable to anything that *seems* to be. Truth consists of two parts: that which is given and that which is accepted. In "The Story of the Trickster's Song," Iktomi and the ducks created a truth: that his sticks were sacred songs. Iktomi wanted the ducks to believe because he was hungry, while the ducks wanted to believe because they wanted to dance. That truth lasted only until one duck opened his eyes and realized yet another truth: Iktomi was killing them and they would all die if they didn't flee. If the ducks had remained skeptical, the momentary truth would not have come about; all the ducks would have lived and Iktomi would have walked away hungry.

We Lakota have heard Iktomi sing several times. At the Fort Laramie Treaty Council of 1851, as thousands upon thousands of white emigrants made their way along the Oregon Trail from Missouri to Oregon and passed through Lakota territory, the United States peace commissioners told us, "They are only passing through and need only as much room as the width of their wagon wheels."

The Fort Laramie Treaty of 1868 established the Great Sioux Reservation—the entire western half of the current state of South Dakota—for "as long as the sun shall rise, as long as the rivers shall flow, as long as the grasses shall grow."

The truth is sometimes painful, but without it there is only illusion. The truth is we Lakota still walk the face of the Earth. The truth is we survived traumatic change and are wiser and stronger because of it. The illusion is that we were defeated by a stronger, better, more moral people with more God-given rights than we had. The truth is we were overwhelmed by numbers: more people with more guns needing more and more of what we had. The illusion is that we are a conquered people. The truth is that we are survivors; we took on the worst that our "conquerors" could throw at us and we are still standing. The illusion is that we are part of the past—something to be studied, analyzed, measured, dissected, and ultimately judged. The truth is we are still a viable culture with traditions, customs, and values that have stood the severest tests.

We all have our truths, some easier to accept than others. The L train is always late; prairie gumbo is bottomless after a hard rain; one brother-in-law is a geek and the other believes he's a saint; commuting sucks; my parents hate me because I'm sixteen; my sixteen-year-old hates me because she's sixteen; a one-sided love affair is the pits; the Minnesota Vikings broke my heart—again; I can't live without my wife. But when all is said and done there is only one truth that is unwavering. It has endured and will always endure because it will stand unabashedly and without apology. That truth is death, and it is the one that is avoided and most feared by American society. But it should be the standard for truth against which all others are measured. And we will find that nothing can compare with its honesty and faithfulness.

Death is a taboo subject, generally speaking, consistently referred to euphemistically as the Grim Reaper, the cold night, or the wages of sin. There is rarely casual conversation among non-Indians about death or dying. Any references to it are made in hushed and apprehensive tones. A visit to any mortuary or cemetery is a confirmation of the general state of denial about death in American society. Funeral directors sell coffins that will "protect your loved one for ages to come." Stone or cement crypts and mausoleums are used for the same reason: to deny death as long as possible.

Logically, we are at least apprehensive about anything we don't know. Most people fear death because they don't know it, or they know the wrong things about it.

No matter how much we deny it or try to avoid it, death touches us sooner or later when a friend or a loved one dies. After we mourn and grieve the loss, many of us become angry at death as if it were an interloper, a thief in the night, a villain, or a killer. Death does not kill. Disease, accidents, rage, old age, stupidity, among others, are killers. Death is only part of the process of life.

The truth about death is simple. It will happen. Nothing is more inevitable, no matter how vigorously we deny it or fight it. Death will come for us regardless of how powerful, famous, rich, beautiful, influential, irreverent, or lowly we are. There is no way to fight it. We can fight to live, but we will always lose the fight with death. Thinking of death in those terms creates the illusion that it is an enemy, but it isn't our enemy; it is, when all is said and done, our truest friend.

The most profound and reassuring truth about death is that it is a part of life. Life begins with birth and ends with death. With no other journey you travel can you know how it will end. We begin dying the moment we are born, which means living well is dying well. That is the truest measure of any being.

The final—and perhaps the greatest—truth about death is that it is the great equalizer; it connects all living beings to its truth. Every form of life shares with us the same journey that begins with birth and ends with death. No one being or species, not the most powerful, nor the most arrogant, nor the wisest will ever alter that truth.

There are many certainties and even more illusions masquerading as truth, nothing short of living and learning will enable us to know the difference. The first chieftain accepted the truth he heard and reacted to it with the truth of his own character, and was rewarded. The Easterner benefited from the wisdom of a man who sought truth in others. Iktomi, on the other hand, presented illusion as truth, and always will.

Truth is what we make it; it serves our own ends. The Lakota regarded the westward migration of the white man as invasion. The white man regarded it as an entitlement. The Lakota look at the land and see a relative. The white man looks at the land and sees a commodity. Neither side is wrong because ultimately all we can do is live our own truth. Sometimes, however, one truth hides another. Beware of Iktomi.

A woman was suddenly stricken with an illness that ultimately was diagnosed as terminal. Though she could reconcile with her own death, she was most concerned for her children. One day, when she could count her life in days, she asked all four of her children to spend the afternoon with her in the hospice. Before they came she was bathed and dressed and had her hair fixed. She was very weak, and the strain of sitting, not to mention the ever-present pain, drained what little energy she had.

The children spent the afternoon with their mother as she had asked. During the visit she sat in a chair and chatted as if nothing were wrong. The afternoon passed pleasantly and uneventfully. When it was time for her children to leave, the woman gave each one a hug and a smile. The moment her children left the room, the woman collapsed from the pain and she died that night.

Months afterward the four children gathered together and the topic of conversation soon turned to the last day they spent with their mother. All of them were grateful that their last moments with her had been wonderful, and they all agreed that their final images of her would never be forgotten. But one expressed some disappointment.

"I know mom was in terrible pain, but she acted as if there were nothing wrong. Why couldn't she be truthful with us?' he wondered.

"Oh, but she was," replied the oldest daughter. "The pain wasn't the truth we should remember. The truth we should remember is the strength and the love she had in order to set it aside for those few hours."

My maternal grandfather gave me a similar gift before he died on March 4, 1975, in the small duplex apartment he and my grandmother lived in. In his final days my grandmother and I sensed that his time was near; he was growing weaker by the hour. She was definitely handling the situation with much more grace than I was. I know my grandfather sensed my pain and turmoil no matter how well I thought I'd disguised it. One morning he gamely took a few sips of tea as I held his cup. Then he touched my hand and, for a moment, I felt his enormous strength of spirit. He spoke, and though his voice was weak, it was clear: *"Takoja, maka wiconi kin hecena kte lo."*

"Grandson, life goes on," he said.

He helped me face one truth by reminding me of another. Of all the gifts he ever gave me, that was the greatest.

8

Compassion

Waunsilapi (wah-un-shee-lah-pee)

To care, to sympathize

✚ The Story of the Eagle

Some of our elders like to tell of how our people came up out of a hole in the Earth, in the southern edge of the Black Hills. That's a creation story. This one I'm about to tell you is a re-creation story. And it wouldn't have a good, happy ending if there were no compassion in the world.

Long ago the people were living in a land of many lakes. In the forests there were many animals, such as deer, elk, and moose, to hunt for food and clothing. The lakes were filled with fish of all kinds, and ducks and geese as well. The people were strong; their enemies were afraid of them and so there was peace. Life was very good.

Then came a particularly hard winter; the snow was deep. It came early and stayed long. All the snow finally melted in May, the Moon of Berries Ripening. Summer brought much rain and the lakes and rivers began to fill. The rains kept falling.

The people knew that the wet season always passed. They patched their round bark-and-thatch lodges to keep the water from leaking in and waited for the rains to let up. But they didn't. The lakes and rivers filled more and more until they all overflowed their banks, yet the rains kept falling. The skies stayed dark and cloudy.

The waters rose higher and higher, chasing the people out of their lodges. They found higher ground and made new lodges, but the water kept coming. Soon there was no rest from the great flood; the people had to keep moving to the high hills and ridges. Even the animals fled from the waters.

Food became scarce because the hunters couldn't hunt. Many belongings were lost to the rising waters. Because there was no dry wood for fires, the people were cold. The first among them to die were the old ones who were too weak to fight the cold and hunger. Soon many people became ill with a coughing sickness. Some grew weak and died because there was no medicine to help them. Then the winds came.

Out of the north came the winds, angry and vengeful. They whipped the floods into a mean-spirited, dark being that sought out the people as they tried to flee, dragging them down into its cold darkness. Within days all but one of the people were dead.

A young woman clung to the rocks of a high hill. She had started climbing with her family, but the wind-driven flood had taken them all. Now she was alone, hungry and cold and dizzy with grief, huddling in the rocks waiting to die. Weakened by hunger and sadness, she fell asleep and slept for several days.

The winds that had turned the flood into a frenzy also chased away the rain clouds. For the first time in nearly a month the sun bathed the land with its healing, soothing warmth. The great winds went away and in their place came gentle breezes that caressed the land with their softer breath.

The great flood was over, but it left death in its passing. Broken and uprooted trees, torn hillsides, and flattened grasses and shrubs were its trail. From the high hill the young woman could see what the flood had done. She would never forget that it had taken her mother and father and her brother and sister. It was of no matter to her that the sun was shining and the animals were beginning to return. She was alone. Her plaintive wail of grief rose over the land, causing four-leggeds and wingeds to pause and listen.

The young woman did not leave the hill. Day after day, night after night, she sat overcome with grief, despair, and loneliness, growing weaker and weaker from lack of food and water. One afternoon she awoke to find a great eagle perched on a nearby rock. He was very large with dark brown, almost black feathers. She was frightened because she knew the eagle to be a great hunter with powerful talons that could rip her flesh, and she had no way to defend herself.

The young woman was drawn to the eagle's soft brown eyes. He looked at her with curiosity. She waited, suddenly sensing that there was no danger. Then the eagle spoke.

"I have seen that you are alone," he said.

She began to sob quietly, then stopped. "Yes," she replied. "The flood took my family; it took all of my people, the two-leggeds. I am alone."

"You are sad. I heard you weeping."

"My family is gone. My people are gone. There is only me and all I have is sadness. It stays with me day and night."

"Then I will be your friend," the eagle said. "Tell me what I can do for you."

"You can do nothing," she lamented. "I am alone. I will die alone."

"That is not true," he replied. "Look around. Your relatives, the four-leggeds; the wingeds like me; and the crawlers: They are here. We are all here."

"But my people are gone. I am the last," she sobbed. "There is no one like me left. So I am waiting to die, to rejoin my people."

"If you die, there will be no more like you on the Earth. There will be nothing but emptiness where your kind once lived. That cannot be. You must live." He stretched his wings and rose in the air.

"Where are you going?" she asked. "Are you leaving me?"

"Only to bring you food," he told her. "I will return."

And he did, bringing a large fish.

"I must make a fire to cook this," she said. "I cannot eat this without cooking it."

"What do you need for fire?" he asked.

"Wood," she said. "Dry wood."

The eagle, of course, could fly very fast, and after several flights to the forest he had collected a large pile of wood for her. The young woman first built a fire starter of wood and cord, then started a fire and cooked the fish. Even a small bite seemed to give her strength; she could feel it flowing through her. All the while the eagle had been sitting back, for he was afraid of the fire.

"You two-leggeds can do a very powerful thing," he said. "You can make fire. But, of course, we wingeds and four-leggeds do not need such a thing."

"Yes. Fire cooks our food so we can eat it. It keeps us warm. There is nothing like a warm fire to chase away the darkness. A good fire is like a good friend."

The eagle brought more wood so she could have a fire through the night and stay warm. In the morning when she awoke he was gone, but her fire was still smoldering. She built up her fire and wondered where he was. For a time he had eased her loneliness and she was grateful. As the morning wore on and he did not return, she thought he had only been a dream. Yet there was the fire and the dried-out skin of the fish.

He returned in the middle of the day, this time with a rabbit. "This is a fine day," he said. "It is good to be alive."

The young woman was glad for the eagle's return. She skinned the rabbit, cooked it, and ate as he watched with great interest.

"There is a fine valley toward where the sun goes down—a good place to build a lodge. There is water and it is sheltered from the cold winter wind. Perhaps you should go there," he said.

"No," she replied, "I am here, and I will stay here. I can build a lodge here, if that is what I want to do."

The eagle could see that her sadness was great. He knew also that she would always be sad because she was the last of her kind. He had flown far over the lakes and valleys, but he had found no other two-leggeds. She would grow old and die alone.

He continued to bring her food and firewood day after day. And he would circle over her hill watching for any danger. Once he chased a bear away from the hill, swooping down again and again.

She grew stronger with each passing day and began to worry about her appearance. She brushed off her dress and made a comb to do her hair. Before the flood she had been the loveliest young woman in many villages, and young men had come from near and far to court her. Now, of course, she was the most beautiful young woman anywhere.

One day while waiting for the eagle, she climbed to the very top of her hill. From there she saw across a wide valley and many lakes. There was beauty all around; in time the scars from the great flood would be no more. But what could she do alone? she wondered. Like any young woman she had dreamed of marrying a fine, handsome young man and having children. They would live not far from her mother and father's lodge in their village by the lake. He would hunt and she would keep their lodge and they would grow old together. Now she was standing on a hill, a cold, terrible truth within her. She was the last of her kind. What was she to do?

One of the tiny black specks in the sky above began to grow larger and larger, and soon she heard the rush of wind under the great wings of the eagle. He landed. She marveled at the spread of his mighty wings and the power in them. But he also had a different power, the power to chase away her loneliness.

"What am I to do?" she asked. "Without you I would have nothing. If only I was an eagle, I would fly with you. I could see what you see from so high in the sky. And I would not be the only one of my kind."

"Come," he said, "we shall fly. Grab my legs as I rise into the air."

She did and they rose from the hill. She was afraid at first and she hung on very tight. But as they soared upward she saw the Earth as she had never seen it before, and she trembled in awe. She felt powerful as everything on the Earth grew smaller. It was a sight she could never have imagined. Though the things on the Earth—trees, hills, lakes, and rivers—grew smaller as they went higher, the Earth itself grew larger, and the young woman was humbled by the wondrous sight of it.

They flew until her arms became tired, but she was reluctant to return to the hill.

"Thank you," she said, "I envy what you are."

"I am your friend," he replied, "and always will be."

Their friendship became stronger. He brought her food, and she scratched pictures of him on the rocks. Every day she ventured farther and farther from her camp and was soon talking about building a lodge somewhere, perhaps on the very top of the hill. The eagle saw that the young woman was smiling more often. Still, he could see sadness in her eyes.

On one fine day in late summer the eagle soared on the winds high above the young woman's hill. Autumn was on the way and winter would not be far behind. Already some cold breezes were coming from the north. The young woman needed to prepare for winter or she would perish. He was troubled.

"Grandfather," he called out, "You who are most powerful, why have you not seen to her well-being?" he asked.

"I have done so," came back a voice. "I have sent you to her."

"I have helped her because she is needful and a fine being," replied the eagle. "I can only bring her food. I cannot give her what she truly needs. She needs others of her kind."

"There is a way," the voice replied.

"Tell me, Grandfather," the eagle said. "I will help her in any way I can."

"You are a fine being, too; you have a kind heart and you are deserving of your place in the Great Circle of Life," said the voice. "Few have your power. It would be difficult to lose your place, for that is what must happen if you truly want to help the two-legged."

"I do not understand, Grandfather."

"To help her you must become a two-legged. If you do, you will never ride the winds again. You will never again see the Earth from above the highest mountains. The choice is yours. You can become a two-legged and as male and female you can together give to the Earth more of her kind. Or you can remain as you are."

The eagle was very quiet that night as he sat with the young woman. He was troubled. She saw that his brown eyes had lost their usual sparkle. "Is there something on your mind?" she asked.

"Yes," he replied. "I must go away. There is much I have to think about."

"You will return?" she asked. "I could not bear it if you were lost to me."

"I will return," he promised. "No matter what happens, I will always be your friend. I will bring you food before I leave. Stay on the hill; do not wander far," he cautioned.

The next day the young woman climbed to the top of the hill and watched the sky. There were many hawks circling and a few eagles. She wondered which one of those high, black specks was her friend. The next day was the same, and the day after that. She was impatient for his return because loneliness stalked her like an enemy in the night.

The eagle soared higher than he had ever flown and saw more of the Earth than he ever seen. It was a sight he never wanted to forget.

"Grandfather," he called out. "I am here."

"Grandson," the voice replied, "I know what is in your heart. You have been troubled for these many days. Yet you have made a choice."

"Yes," said the eagle. "I know what I must do."

"The choice you make is a road you can never turn back from," said the voice.

"There are still many of my kind," said the eagle. "She is only one, and she cannot be the last of her kind. The Earth and everything on it would feel the loss. I can see no other way."

"So be it," said the voice. "I tell you this. Two-leggeds will find a place in their hearts for your kind. They will hold you high."

Summer was ending, the young woman knew. Cold breezes came down from the north. She walked the hillside to gather wood for her fire. Now and then she looked up at the sky, but as yet he had not returned.

"Do you wait for someone?" came a voice from behind her.

It was a familiar voice, one she knew very well. He had returned. The young woman turned with a smile, which became a frown. She could see no one.

"I am here," said the familiar voice. The young woman nearly fainted as a tall, handsome young man stepped from behind a rock.

"How can this be?" she cried. "I thought all of us were taken by the flood except for me!"

"That is true," said the young man.

"Then where do you come from?"

"From the sky," the young man replied.

The young woman was shocked into silence and disbelief. Yet the voice of the young man was familiar; it was the voice of the eagle. Pushing aside her confusion and fear, she stepped closer. There was something familiar in those deep, brown eyes, also.

"Remember the day we flew together?" he asked. "I took you up far above the Earth."

"It cannot be!" she cried. "It is you!"

"I promised I would return, and so I have. Are you not happy to see me?"

The young woman ran and fell into his embrace, feeling something she thought could never be. Yet she felt something else as well: Each time she came near to him thereafter she felt as though she were soaring.

Before that winter they built a lodge at the edge of a forest and in time became mother and father to many children, and to a new race of two-leggeds. She told her children who their father was and what he had been. They would watch the sky as the great eagles flew. They were, of course, watching their relatives. They taught their children who taught their children, and so on, to do the same.

Perhaps now you understand why eagle feathers are sacred to us. To this day we Lakota revere the great eagles, and each time we see one in the sky we pause to speak our thanks to those relatives for their compassion.

Take Their Hand

Without compassion darkness would rule the world. Poverty, despair, and hopelessness caused by war, natural disaster, or indifference are as much a part of this life as harmony, success, and prosperity. At some point in our lives most of us find ourselves in need of a place to sleep, money for the rent, or simply the knowledge that someone cares. If you can't remember at least one such moment, you're more fortunate than most of us—or perhaps you're only misleading yourself. The ability to feel compassion is to understand need. When need is not recognized and alleviated, our spirits sink into darkness.

One summer in the mid-1950s when I was nine, in a small town in the northern part of the Rosebud Sioux Indian Reservation, there was a death in a Lakota family. An infant had died. On the day of the funeral I accompanied my grandmother to the family's home above an old store in town. The parents were very poor and couldn't afford a casket or the services of a mortician. It was stiflingly hot that day and not a breath of air moved in the small rooms the family occupied, though every window was propped open. On the kitchen table was a cardboard container—not much bigger than a shoe box and lined with white crepe paper. In it was the body of the dead baby, dressed in its finest clothes. My first impression was that it was simply asleep. A few relatives and friends of the family were gathered in the sparsely furnished rooms. No one spoke as we entered. There was a painful, heavy silence.

The baby's mother was someone I knew—a relative on my grandmother's side, as a matter of fact. Dressed in black she sat next to the table, guarding—it seemed—the tiny form in the makeshift casket. The older daughter, about my age, sat next to her mother. My grandmother shook hands with each of them, then turned to me. "Take their hands," she instructed. So I did, very self-consciously. I took the hand of the mother, then the daughter. It was one of my first lessons in showing compassion.

I stood next to my grandmother, who had taken a chair offered her as she quietly wiped away the tears sliding down her face with a white handkerchief. Years later I realized that she was not just consoling the family of the dead baby, but actually feeling their pain and loss, taking some of it—perhaps as much as possible—upon herself.

That is compassion, simply and profoundly: the sharing of someone else's dilemma, pain, or loss—caring enough to take some of the burden or provide relief so that the aggrieved or injured person does not have to bear it alone.

In one of the numerous indiscriminate and heartrending,

situations of combat—which happen in a split second but impose consequences for a lifetime—a young marine suddenly saw his lower right arm fly away from him amid the unfettered, noisy violence of an intense firefight in the Quang Tri province of South Vietnam. He stared in shock as it landed a few feet away in a swatch of saw grass. In the next few seconds the unseen enemy broke off the engagement and withdrew. In the eerie, tense silence that followed, the marine stared numbly at the stump of his arm. He had been the only casualty in the brief, intense encounter. As the corpsman rushed to administer aid, the marine fainted. Later, two fellow marines carried him on a makeshift litter as he lay in shock, groggy from morphine. Walking next to the litter was another young marine carrying the severed arm. The sight of it, strangely enough, seemed to comfort the wounded boy before he lapsed into a morphine-induced sleep. In the time it took the rifle platoon to rendevous with a medevac helicopter, the wounded marine's buddy faithfully carried the arm. In other circumstances this could have been considered macabre behavior by most people. But in this instance it was an act of compassion.

Compassion is often the only remedy when something assaults our bodies and minds and causes our spirits to slip into darkness. No one is immune from affliction, and often enough we find ourselves unable to bear it alone. In all probability, no one can completely take away the pain of our despair or the grief of losing a loved one, but the fact that someone who's experienced the same loss mourns with us is comforting. The sense of comfort comes from the realization that we are not alone in our darkest hour. The physical act of "taking their hands" in the moment of grief, despair, or need is the outward manifestation of compassion. Often no words are—or need to be—spoken to coincide with that simple act because it speaks volumes. It says, "I've been there."

The young marine who carried his buddy's severed arm for

the six or seven miles offered no words of explanation to anyone. He didn't need to; he simply and instinctively performed
an act of compassion because the moment required it.

My grandmother had lost her younger sister to Spanish influenza when they were nineteen and eighteen years old. She
knew all too well the pain that death can cause, and she wasn't
about to let that young mother bear her loss alone.

Known for her caring and wise counsel, Grandma was always
asked to say a few words at gatherings like wakes, funerals, or
memorial feasts (in which the passing of a loved one is remembered). Invariably she talked about the necessity of compassion,
and her advice was simple: "When there are people in need,"
she would say, "take their hands."

It is an unfortunate fact of life that "happily ever after"
doesn't occur often enough; on the other side of the ledger is
the fortunate fact that compassion lives within most of us. Some
of us are more willing to demonstrate it, but those who can't or
won't should reassess themselves to determine whether they've
been able to endure difficulties absolutely and entirely on their
own. I know I haven't: My parents and grandparents have helped
me through moments of anguish and confusion when my own
emotional resources were not sufficient. My best friend, a writer,
has willingly given of his money and ear without batting the
proverbial eye. Were it not for him, my family and I would have
been stranded in a big city without money. This friend, who lost
his father recently, has been a comforting listener who helped
soothe the turmoil surrounding my father's losing battle with
cancer. Friends from the east have helped with generous loans
to ease our financial burden without asking, "When can you pay
us back?" Unintentionally, my relatives and friends have taught
me how to be compassionate because they themselves were, and
are. And the best way to thank them and honor them for this
gift is to be compassionate myself to those who may need me to
"take their hands."

Difficulties and problems are part of life and they fall upon us individually and collectively. And sometimes the simple *hope* of compassion, without it being actively demonstrated, can get us through a hard time. In the 1930s a rural mail carrier on the Rosebud Reservation learned that lesson. He was near the end of his route on a cool, cloudy day in late March and had one more letter to deliver, to the last stop on his route. Two farms in between that normally had mail daily had none this day, so he decided to take a cut across a seldom-used pasture trail so that he could finish his route early and have time to do chores at home. Snow started falling and rapidly turned into a thick white curtain that reduced visibility to only a few yards. Though the mail carrier probably could have driven his regular route blind-folded, he was not very familiar with the cut-across. He made a wrong turn and felt his old Model T Ford, atop the slippery, wet snow, slide sideways down an incline and then come to rest at the bottom of a gully. Try as he might, he couldn't coax the vehicle back up the slope. The heavy wet snow had turned the hillside into greasy mud.

The mail carrier considered the situation and his options. He was at the bottom of a gully in the middle of a March snowstorm, some forty yards below a pasture trail only infrequently used by vehicular traffic. As a lifelong resident of the northern Plains, he knew that March snowstorms were unpredictable. He could walk to the highway that was about two miles away, but if the snowfall turned into a blizzard, he would be in the open without adequate clothing. After a few minutes he decided have a look at the gully and the slopes, entertaining a faint hope that there was a gentler slope with less of an incline that his Model T could climb. Then his spirits soared when he remembered there was a set of tire chains in the rumble seat. Stepping down from the car, however, he slipped on the wet snow and fell heavily, twisting his knee and jamming his shoulder.

Painfully regaining his feet, he opened the rumble seat to verify that the tire chains were there, which was so. But his twisted knee prevented him from exploring the gully and the surrounding slopes, and his shoulder—which had been numb at first—suddenly erupted with pain. His right arm hung oddly and he quickly determined that he had broken his collarbone. He retreated back into the car and reconsidered his options.

His knee was swelling, his shoulder throbbed, and the snow was still falling—and no one knew where he was. His liabilities were the weather and his injuries. His assets were his car and the tire chains. But in order for the chains to be useful and effective, they had to be placed on the rear wheels. In order to do that he had to jack up each wheel and clamp the chains in place. With a broken collarbone and a swollen knee that could barely take his weight, putting on tire chains seemed an impossible task. The sensible course, he surmised, would simply be to wait. The snowfall would stop eventually, and when he didn't get home, his wife would worry and contact the neighbor. But that neighbor lived four miles from them and she would have to walk, since they had only the one vehicle. And even if there was a search this evening or tomorrow, he was at the bottom of a gully below a seldom-used pasture trail. That a search would be initiated eventually he was certain: His neighbors were caring, compassionate people, and there was a slight chance they would search the cut-across he had taken. His best hope was to put on the tire chains and try to climb the slope to that trail before the snow became too deep.

Faith in his neighbors' sense of concern for his welfare drove him to make the attempt, but the narrow base of the jack sank into the mud or slipped sideways. After several attempts he succumbed to the futility of putting on the chains with only one good arm. He reconsidered his approach.

Inside the car were a wool blanket, gloves, a half-eaten slice of meat in waxed paper, matches, and a small kerosene lantern—and a feeling that his neighbors would search for him when he was seriously past due. Checking his pocket watch, he knew that his wife would be expecting him to arrive home about then. He was hardly ever late, even in bad weather, so she was certain to worry after an hour passed. An hour after that would be sundown; perhaps by then she or his son would walk to the neighbor's farm. That would take nearly an hour. He calculated that he had at least three hours before someone would start driving his mail route to search for him. He had at least that much time to walk back to the turnoff to the cut-across, a little over two miles in distance. But the snowfall was not abating and by now had covered the pasture trail; he would have to rely on memory to stay on it.

He faced a moment of indecision. It would be sensible to remain with the car; it was shelter. He could keep warm through the night by lighting the lantern. But if the weather turned nasty, as it had been known to do in March, it might prevent a search and he could be stranded for days.

He made his decision. He folded the blanket and draped it over his injured shoulder to keep it warm and then put on his coat. The slice of meat he stuck in his pocket along with his matches. Slipping on his gloves and cap, he buttoned his coat and stepped out into the falling snow, sensing that the air was growing colder.

After half an hour of laborious, painful step-by-step climbing, and several slips, he gained the top of the hill. Both the twisted knee and broken shoulder were throbbing. He cast about in small circles until he found the shallow depressions beneath the snow that told him the trail was there. Then he had to guess which way was east, back toward the turnoff. If he guessed wrong, he had four miles to walk to the highway as opposed to two.

How he managed to stay on the trail he never knew. He had to pause often to dig through the snow with his good leg to find the shallow depressions of the trail. Though the effort kept him warm, it slowed him considerably. Three hours after he started he reached the fence line. After following it to the right for a distance he couldn't find the gate. Turning back, he followed the fence again. After another half hour of hobbling he found the gate. He walked onto the highway surface but found no indication that any vehicle had passed. He retreated to the gatepost and sat down under a tent he built for himself by attaching his shoulder blanket to the post. It kept the snow from soaking him all the more. He suddenly realized that his jaw was sore from clenching it tightly against the pain of his knee and broken collarbone. Fumbling with his good arm, he managed to light the lantern to warm himself beneath the makeshift tent. As he leaned back against the post he heard the *pop-pop* of a vehicle motor.

Struggling painfully to his feet, he hobbled to the road and waited with the lantern in his hand. Out of the snow appeared his neighbor's truck with his wife in the cab beside the driver.

There was one constant factor each time the mail carrier told his story in the years that followed. "I knew I could count on the compassion of my neighbors," he said. That was what drove him to leave the shelter of his car. Sometime during that night the snowfall turned into a full-blown blizzard, so it might have been days before he received proper medical attention for his injuries. As it was, several weeks lapsed before his Model T could be dug out of the gully. Until he died the mail carrier who believed in the kindness of his neighbors never hesitated to respond anytime day or night, whenever one of them needed his help.

9

Bravery

Woohitike—(wo-oh-hee-tee-keh)

Having or showing courage

✚ The Story of Defender

Long ago our people survived by hunting and by fighting when necessary. So Lakota boys had to learn the skills to be providers as well as protectors—hunters as well as warriors. For skills like making weapons, tracking, and shooting bows and arrows a boy needed good hands and a good eye.

It was easy to see which boy was good with the bow or which was good at tracking. But to be a good hunter and warrior it was also necessary to be brave, and that could not always be seen in a boy. We believed that it was in everyone to be brave, but we also knew that boys had to be given the chance to learn they could be brave.

My grandmother told me a story about one boy long ago. His boyhood name was *Hoka,* the badger. Though he was named for a ferocious animal, he was a quiet child. In fact, he hardly ever cried when he was a baby. In time he would earn another name.

Hoka was eager to learn. By the time he was twelve he could make arrows better than most grown men. By the time he was fourteen he was deadly with his bow. He could look at a track and know what animal had passed by and when. He was quiet and often went off alone, so his father worried. One of Hoka's uncles said it was time to see what the boy was made of.

One day that uncle organized a hunting party and invited Hoka along. It was customary for a boy on the edge of manhood to be invited along on a hunt or the warpath as a helper. Such a helper did chores around the camp but also was given the chance to learn from the experience.

The hunting party was after elk. A medicine dreamer needed the fine hide of a mature elk to make into a courting robe, and some of the old ones in the village needed fresh meat. So after the proper preparations the hunters departed.

They found a good spot for a hunting camp in a valley thick with cottonwood and oak. Hoka helped to set up the camp while some of the hunters went on a scout. They returned with good news. The next morning, with Hoka carrying the extra weapons, water, and food pouches, the hunters went after their game. They were successful: They returned to camp with two fine elk.

The elk were skinned and butchered. Hoka's uncle said the hunters would go out again the next day and that Hoka would stay behind to guard the camp. Guarding the camp was a big responsibility. Coyotes, wolves, or bears could come after the fresh meat, so someone had to stay behind. More importantly, guarding the camp was the same as defending the village where there were many helpless, like the old ones and the women and children. This was an important lesson for a boy about to become a man.

Soon after sunrise the hunters left, assuring Hoka that they would return by sundown. His uncle reminded the boy that the elk meat would feed many families back in the village, so nothing must happen to it. He reminded him the elk hides for the medicine dreamer had been stretched out to dry and that they were very important as well. Hoka gathered his bow and arrows and promised he would guard the camp.

The camp was well hidden in the oak and cottonwood near the creek, but that also meant an enemy could sneak up close under cover. The meat was hanging from a pole placed in the forks of two young cottonwoods and covered with cut willow branches. Though out of sight, the meat could not be hidden from the keen noses of four-legged meat eaters. Of that Hoka was well aware. Yet the first visitor was not four-legged; it was the loud black and white magpie, an opportunist who quickly announced his discovery to the whole valley. Soon a flock of magpies surrounded the camp.

A well-placed clod of dirt now and then kept the magpies away, but they made themselves a constant nuisance and their loud, screechy calls were no less a bother. Hoka knew that other creatures like the short-tailed cat, the great cat, coyotes, bears, and wolves often followed the loud calls of the magpies. Wolves and coyotes would not attack two-leggeds, but bears and the great cat were another matter. So Hoka kept his weapons close and his eyes on the surrounding trees.

At midmorning Hoka was tiring of throwing dirt clods at the magpies and went to the creek to fill his water pouch. Returning to the camp, he came upon a large track resembling a bear's paw print. He studied it carefully. The print was not deep, but it was large, and Hoka couldn't remember seeing it on his way to the water. Back at camp he strung his bow and put his arrows within easy reach. Bears could be killed with a bow: A few hunters had done it, but they were grown men and much stronger than he, and with stouter bows than his. There were also a few stories of hunters who had been killed or maimed by an angry wounded bear, like the man named Crooked Leg whose ankle had been broken by a bear with one bite. After the charging buffalo, a bear with a hump in his back was the most dangerous four-legged anywhere.

Hoka was more watchful, keeping his eyes and ears open. Only the leaves, grasses, and shrubs were moving with the gentle breeze that flowed through the grove. The only sounds were the loud magpies. He was about to think that the track he had found was old when something scared away the magpies. With loud screeching they flapped away from the grove; other birds fled as well, leaving behind a sudden silence.

Hoka crouched with his bow, his back to a tree, and placed an arrow on the string. Whatever had frightened the magpies had to be something more dangerous than a coyote. The possibilities were not good. Only a ferocious hunter like the gray short-tailed cat, the great yellow cat, the wolf, or a bear could frighten away every other creature.

He listened hard and looked closely all around. There was only the silence and nothing moved, as if the breezes had fled, too. Hoka glanced up at the sun. It was not yet the middle of the day, meaning there was a long wait until sundown and the hunters' return. He was alone against whatever had caused the strange silence.

It dragged on. Perhaps something had just passed through, he hoped. Then he heard a rustling in the brush. Hoka took a position to shoot. He had seen bears at a distance but never up close. Once, while hunting with his father, he had witnessed the great yellow cat take down a deer. It had been very swift and powerful. What was out there among the trees he didn't know, but he imagined he would be able to get off one shot, maybe two.

Once again there was only the silence.

Hoka relaxed a little, but he kept the bow in his hand, the arrow still held on the string. He pressed his back against the tree and slowly swept his gaze all around until he'd completed a circle. Still there was nothing but silence.

He began to consider what to do if a bear or the great cat came for him across the clearing. Both of those four-leggeds were very swift; they could outrun a two-legged easily. One shot was all he would get, if that, and one arrow wouldn't kill any animal that large. The tree next to him was a large cottonwood with high branches. He could climb it high enough to be out of a bear's reach because the humpback bear couldn't climb trees, but the great yellow cat could, easily. Hoka pondered. What was he to do?

He could go and look for the hunters, he thought, but they were counting on him to guard the meat. Hunting wasn't easy; it was hard work requiring much skill and patience. If a bear or a great yellow cat came in and took the meat while he was off looking for the hunters, he would be responsible. Everyone would make fun because it would look like he ran away. Hoka sighed deeply. Clearly, there was nothing to do but defend the camp. Still, he knew very well what a bear or a great yellow cat could do to him. He shuddered at the thought of it. One of the hunters had left behind a lance, so Hoka brought that close. It would be the last thing he would use if his arrows missed, or if he couldn't get off more than two shots.

The rustling came again, this time off to his left. Hoka swung around to shoot but saw nothing. The noise was louder this time. Whatever made it was not a small animal like a badger or a fox. It had to be large.

Something moved, something dark and large, and fast. Hoka caught the movement in the corner of his eye. He gasped and swung around. The dark figure disappeared behind some trees. Hoka waited, trying not to breathe hard because it would spoil his aim if he had to shoot. Now he knew for certain. There *was* something out there! He suddenly realized his heart was thumping against his chest.

Hoka tried to reason past his fear. He guessed it was not a great yellow cat because the cat was a stalker. Its way of hunting was to move in close without being seen and then spring. The thing out there was dark, perhaps black, and not tawny yellow. It could only be a bear. Something was out there and he might have to face it. Remembering the story of the hunter from a village to the north, he preferred to face a bear.

His grandfather had told of a man hunting near the Great Muddy River. The man noticed a great cat watching him. It followed him across a creek, into a forest, and up a tree. The cat was relentless, screaming and growling as it climbed. Somehow the hunter thrust his lance as the cat leaped. It impaled itself and both cat and hunter fell, crashing to the forest floor. That hunter had been very lucky. He lived to tell the story and made a fine bow case and arrow quiver from the cat's hide.

The last thing Hoka wanted to face was the great yellow cat. Truth was he didn't want to face the bear, either, but it seemed as if he would have no choice. His gaze swept the grove all around him once again. His mouth was dry. He removed his shirt so that its sleeves wouldn't get in the way of the bowstring. Taking out three arrows, he stuck them in the ground in front of him and arranged the quiver full of at least twenty arrows at his left hip. Counting the arrow on the string, he calculated four fast shots—if he had time.

A loud thrashing from behind startled him. He whirled and bent his bow, expecting to see some large black thing coming for him. The noise stopped. With bated breath he waited, looking, and listening. Far off to his right came a low, throaty growl. The bear—if it was a bear—had moved swiftly to flank him. Hoka waited; he looked down and realized that he had spilled out all the arrows from his quiver. Hands trembling, he retrieved the shafts and slid them back in. Taking deep breaths to calm himself, he peered into the trees to the right. The thing had moved from left to right, circling him. Perhaps the wise thing was to look ahead to where it might be, he thought. He was right.

Another low, throaty growl floated through the grove. Hoka heard the dogs snarl, too, but this sound seemed to be coming from a deep hole. All he could do was point his half-drawn bow in the direction of the growl. He wished with all his heart that the hunters were back, but sundown was far, far off. How angry would my uncle be, he wondered, if I went to a safer place away from this bear? There was no way to know that, of course, but he was on the verge of running as far and as fast as he could. Then he decided to climb the tree.

In the tree he was still near enough to see anything that came near the meat. If it was a bear, he could try shouting and scaring it away. If that didn't work, he could shoot at it from a safe perch. Gathering the lance and his bow and arrows, Hoka quickly climbed up. He found a good solid fork higher than the height of two men. There he lodged his lance and found a branch to hang his quiver. And he had a better view of the clearing. As he settled in he heard another growl. He swung around in time to see a dark figure scurrying through the brush, circling the camp, it seemed.

Hoka felt safe in the tree. He made certain of his footing and balance and placed an arrow on the bowstring. The dark figure—he was sure it was a bear—stopped in some low shrubs well within bow shot. He would have to shoot between two trees, but he was certain he could hit it from this distance. The dark figure rose from his hiding place slowly. It was a bear, and it appeared to be looking at him! Perhaps a near miss would scare it away, he thought.

Hoka bent his bow, took careful aim, and released. His arrow flashed toward the bear, which ducked out of sight. Hoka thought he heard a cry, a startled grunt of surprise, followed by a thrashing in the shrubs. Then there was silence.

Wounded animals were dangerous, he had been told. He expected the bear to come after him and try to climb the tree. He prepared another arrow and waited. The silence continued.

No more growls, no more movement in the brush. Hoka kept an eye on the place where he last saw the bear, waiting for it to emerge in a fury. Nothing happened. There was no movement anywhere in the grove. Hoka looked around from his high perch. Only a squirrel was moving about in a nearby oak.

He kept his bow at the ready. All he could do was wait and wonder if he had killed the bear with one arrow. It didn't seem likely.

The sun reached the middle of the sky and began its slide down to the western rim of the prairie. Still Hoka waited, reluctant to leave the safety of the tree. He put away his bow and made himself comfortable, settling himself in the fork of two large branches. A magpie flapped his way through the trees and alighted on the branches above the hanging elk meat, sending his raucous call to all his relatives. Hoka breathed a sigh of relief. That could only mean that there was no more danger from the bear.

More and more magpies came until there was a line of the black and white birds on the cut branch holding up the elk meat. Hoka thought to loose an arrow to frighten them off; then he realized they were his sentinels. If any kind of danger approached, they would fly off. And even all those magpies together couldn't carry off the meat. So he let them be.

The afternoon dragged on and the shadows grew longer and longer. Hoka decided to climb down. On the ground he quickly built a fire. The smell of it and the smoke would warn off any animal approaching. The smell of smoke would also let a two-legged enemy know where the camp was, but he decided to take a chance. His friends the magpies were still worrying about the meat, and he was certain they would let him know if anything came close. But he kept his weapons at hand nonetheless.

Hoka was curious about the bear—if it was a bear. The magpies were unafraid so he decided to take a look. At the last moment he grabbed the lance instead of his bow.

Caution guided his every move as he carefully went from tree to tree until he reached the brush where the bear had been hiding. His heart pounding, he climbed a tree for a better look. He saw nothing. Back on the ground he stepped silently through the brush until he found broken stalks and torn up grass, and blood. His arrow had found a mark!

Wisely he retreated to his fire, built it up, and waited. The magpies were still fussing over the elk meat. He couldn't let down his guard now; there was a wounded bear out there somewhere. The hunters! Hoka hoped the bear wouldn't see the hunters and attack them.

A shout startled him. The hunters were returning from the east and the bear had run off to the west. Hoka was relieved—and never so glad to see anyone in his life. A buck deer with large antlers lay across a drag pole pulled by two of the hunters. They all looked tired and Hoka's uncle seemed to be hurt. A questioning glance from Hoka brought out the story.

One of them had shot the buck. In his confusion it ran at their hiding place and trampled Hoka's uncle. It was not a serious injury, Hoka was told, but there was blood.

"All is well here?" asked Hoka's uncle.

"Yes," replied Hoka. "The meat is still hanging there."

"We have been away since this morning. Did anything happen?"

Hoka thought for a moment. He wanted to tell them about the bear, but more than likely they would not believe him. "No," he said. "Nothing happened. Except for the magpies. They are still trying to carry off the meat."

The hunters looked at him and chuckled.

"You have guarded the camp well," one of them said.

Hoka smiled. They did not know how true their words were. "It would be good if we kept watch tonight," he said. "I hear there are bears here."

"Spoken like a true hunter, and a good man," said his uncle. "Yes, we will take turns keeping watch. Bears are very smart and tricky. You never know what they will do, especially if they smell fresh meat."

◇◇◇

Hoka grew into a fine young man. At his naming ceremony his father and his uncle gave him the name *Naicinji,* the Defender. It was a name he never dishonored. Defender was a skilled hunter and a strong warrior. His family was always well fed and dressed, and he saw to the needy as well. As a fighting man he won many war honors, but he was always a quiet man, never boastful. Of that his mother and father were very proud.

Defender courted and won the love of a fine young woman. They were married and she gave birth to a daughter. Defender's uncle came with a gift for his granddaughter. He brought an arrow.

"A bear gave me this," he told the infant, with her mother and father listening, "long, long ago. He received it from one of the bravest young men he had ever met, he said. I give it to you now, Granddaughter. Hold it in your hand and let its spirit pass on to you so that one day you will grow up to be the mother of brave hunters and warriors. It belongs to your father, one of the bravest men I have ever known."

Being Brave

What is bravery? And why is it a requisite virtue?

Many of us believe that the ultimate display of bravery can only happen on the field of battle. Facing the possibility, and sometimes the probability, of death and great bodily harm is without a doubt one of the most daunting realities any human being can confront. Bravery, however, needs to be taken in context because life demands it in so many ways.

In January of 1951 a five-year-old boy on the Rosebud Sioux Reservation was sent on a simple errand of taking a bag full of fresh meat to relatives who lived below the hill from him and his grandparents. It was after dark, though there was a full moon, and the relatives' house was a two-and-a-half-mile walk on new-fallen snow. The boy was familiar with the road. He had been on it many times, but never alone at night.

It was a pleasant evening, for January, with just enough of a nip in the air to make the snow crunch under his feet as he walked. The sky was clear and it was altogether a very beautiful winter night with the proliferation of stars and the moonlight reflecting off the snow. The boy walked easily without the least amount of concern. He switched the cloth bag from one hand to the other and began to swing it back and forth with the rhythm of his walking. Somewhere in the distance a coyote barked, followed by the tremolo cry of a screech owl. Nothing was unfamiliar to the boy, not the coyote or the owl, the starry, moonlit night, the snow, the cold, or the land itself.

Halfway to the relatives' house, however, there arose a slight aberration that caused a tiny inkling of concern. The aberration persisted and the inkling of concern grew to the first symptoms of fear. The boy, as you recall, was swinging the bag of meat back and forth as he walked. At the back end of the swing it unexpectedly touched *something* ever so slightly.

Instantaneously a swirl of thoughts and images flew through the boy's mind, but he didn't dare alter the pattern of his swinging of the bag. Horrendously large, black, hungry things with frothy white fangs and long, curved claws were predominant among the images in his mind. They were obviously after the bag of meat first, and after that . . . The boy had two choices, as he saw it. He could drop the bag and run or he could run with the bag. The second choice seemed the more honorable because his grandmother had impressed upon him the importance of delivering the meat to the waiting relatives.

Even as he pondered his choices, the bag was still touching *something* at the back end of the swing. The indescribable black things were not going away without a meal.

An inspiration flashed through his mind like a shooting star, and before he could stop himself he was acting on it. He swung the bag backward as hard as he could, after which he intended to run faster than he ever had in his five years on Earth. But he didn't have to.

A sharp yelp surprised and startled him and he nearly ran anyway, but he recognized the yelper. It was his dog. The indescribably relieved boy hugged his dog and they finished the chore and arrived home to report an uneventful journey.

◇◇◇

In that same year a young man from the Winnebago tribe of eastern Nebraska, Sergeant Mitchell Red Cloud, was an American infantry soldier in South Korea. His rifle squad was engaged in an intense firefight with a larger North Korean unit and forced to withdraw. Sergeant Red Cloud took up a rearguard position and protected the withdrawal of his squad. He fired at the oncoming enemy and drew its return fire at himself, thereby enabling his squad to reach a safe position. In the process Sergeant Red Cloud's position was overrun by the North Koreans and he was killed. He was posthumously awarded the Congressional Medal of Honor.

There is no comparison between the courage of a five-year-old boy and the immeasurable bravery of an infantry soldier who lays down his life for his fellow soldiers. Yet it is a safe bet that somewhere in his childhood Mitchell Red Cloud faced a defining moment when he had to "defend the camp" and learn that he was capable of bravery when it was necessary.

Fortunately, most of us won't have to experience combat, but we will have to cope with life's challenges and overcome its obstacles. Schoolyard bullies, rush hour traffic, injury, illness, indifference, our own sense of inadequacy, unemployment, indecision, racial prejudice, physical disability—the list is practically endless. There is a nearly constant assault on our sense of well-being and self-esteem, not to mention an occasional or even frequent threat of bodily harm.

Such is life.

In the 1950s and 1960s yet another challenge swept into the lives of Native Americans on reservations, as if the whole stigma of reservations wasn't challenging enough. We were constantly reminded by certain elements of mainstream American society—missionaries and educators being the most vociferous—that our only course to happiness was to become white in every way possible. Hard work, they told us, was the answer. Buy into the American dream, they advised. The scary part was they had a plan as well—the Employment Assistance Program, otherwise known as "relocation."

The rationale behind the Bureau of Indian Affairs relocation program was not totally without merit. In order for Indian males to support their families, they needed a trade and work experience. Relocation would give them both by placing them in areas where they could learn a trade while supporting they families. But several factors ensured the program's failure.

Indian families who signed up for relocation were moved from their reservations to cities like Cleveland, Minneapolis, Los Angeles, Denver, Oakland, Dallas, and so on. Most had never been near a large city and few knew what to expect. Pitifully little, if any, effort had been made to prepare them for life in a city. Culture shock, to put it mildly, was their first reaction, but the worst aspects were substandard living conditions—in slums, less than a living wage, and lack of appropriate follow-up support by the BIA. It isn't difficult to understand, then, that the first thought in the minds of relocated families was to get home the fastest way possible.

Although there were a few success stories, the relocation program did not accomplish its purpose. Most of the families went home to their reservations without finishing the program. More than a few did it by hitchhiking. Almost every Native American family in the country had its brush with relocation, and horror stories abound. Confusion was its primary consequence, as well as yet another reason to distrust the federal government—especially the Bureau of Indian Affairs. Relocation turned out to be just another in a long and continuing list of challenges to be met, something else to be survived. It was the bear that attacked our camp.

Such is life.

◇◇◇

The Turtle Lady was one of those who lived life bravely. She died a few years ago and as far as I know she never married. She was known as the Turtle Lady because she kept a turtle in her handbag. She also had turtle charms and amulets. It was hard to say where she called home. She was known far and wide by Indians and whites alike because she walked everywhere, a woman alone on the highways and back roads of a rural state. Over the years she crisscrossed the state of South Dakota from one reservation to the next, visiting relatives. Like a turtle she traveled slowly but always managed to reach her destination.

Her name was Elsie Flood and she greeted everyone with a smile. And everyone who knew her worried about her personal safety because of her chosen lifestyle. Given that some elements of the state's population were not kindly disposed toward Indians, there was reason for Elsie's friends and relatives to worry. To my knowledge, though she had one or two minor incidents, Elsie was never seriously injured. I'll always admire her because she was quiet and unassuming, the epitome of courtesy, and bravery.

So was Mac Cash, who was twenty-two when he died of leukemia. This young man was a student of mine who had graduated from the same high school I did. He was one of the brightest young men I've ever known and one of the best foosball players around, but I was most impressed with the dignity and courage he exhibited while he knew he was dying. One expects that kind of strength of spirit from elderly people: It is an affirmation of the lives we should strive to live. Dignity and courage from a young person facing imminent death, however, is an inspiration.

There are at least two inspiring members of my family. In 1989, my sister Barbara's daughter Kim, nearing her seventeenth birthday, died in a car crash (see Dedication). Few things in life are as absolutely heartbreaking as losing a child, few things as challenging. Whatever doesn't kill you will make you stronger, it is said. Barbara found ways to be strong and courageous. She will always have my admiration for that and my undying gratitude for giving me an example to follow.

My father, Joseph Marshall II, was a soldier in the Eighth Army Air Corps. He saw combat during some of the mop-up operations on the island of Okinawa in 1945. Before that, as a twelve-year-old boy, he faced his first test of bravery and passed with flying colors. He became lost in a blizzard with his horse while bringing home supplies for his family. By allowing the horse to find his own way home, my father learned about trust as well as bravery. But his most daunting challenge was cancer.

A tumor was removed from his colon in May of last year. That was followed by chemotherapy treatments for several months. The process is not curative; it is only to prolong a life threatened by terminal illness. At the age of seventy-seven he faced the toughest challenge anyone can be given with the quiet dignity and courage of one who is no stranger to adversity. Years ago my father faced alcoholism and defeated it. He couldn't defeat the cancer, but he taught all of us how to be brave. He died April 14, 2001.

Bravery is a requisite virtue because life demands it. Whether it's cancer, a broken heart, a lost opportunity, a bad business deal, an approaching hurricane, a tough decision, or a dark alley, life will continually throw challenges at us. Any challenge is also an invitation, a standing invitation.

The ancient Lakota hunter/warrior handcrafted his own bows from ash wood. The strongest bows are made from dry, well-seasoned wood. There are two ways to acquire the kind of wood necessary. The conventional way is to find a young ash tree of the proper height and width, harvest it, and let it dry and cure for at least five years. But the hunter/warrior was always on the lookout for a mature ash tree that had been struck by lightning. Such a tree had been dried and cured in an instant by the awesome power of lightning, and any bows made from it were by far the strongest. Lightning-struck ash trees were rare, but they were preferred because they had suffered ultimate adversity, and ultimate adversity produces ultimate strength.

Such is life.

I believe we all have it in us to be brave, that each one of us can defend the camp when it's necessary. Life will give us the opportunity, issuing the invitation to the contest, and as time goes on we will be shaped and strengthened by our challenges. Whether we win each time or not, we will be tempered by adversity.

◇◇◇

Soldiers dressed in blue had ridden against the south end of the village in the early afternoon, on a hot day during the Moon of Cherries Ripening (June), and were turned back—outfought by the warriors who had responded to the danger. A new danger came from the north end as another group of soldiers tried to cross the Greasy Grass River and attack the camp. They were driven back as well and were being chased away toward the north.

There was much confusion and noise in the large village that stretched for over two miles along the west side of the river. As was the usual procedure when a village was attacked, women and children fled, retreating from the attack. One old woman was concerned about the young men in her family who were in the thick of the fighting across the river. She took her young granddaughter's hand and together they waded across the river. Warriors rushing past them to join the fight called for them to go back to the village, but they didn't.

They gained a small plateau and could plainly see the fighting. A brown cloud of dust hung over the Earth, and the firing from the soldiers' and warriors' guns was one continuous noise. They could see the soldiers running and falling as the Lakota and Sahiyela (Northern Cheyenne) drove them relentlessly.

The old woman stopped on a low, sharp rise as the soldiers gained a high hill to the northeast. Suddenly a group of soldiers broke off and ran in her direction, but just as quickly they were cut down to a man by the advancing warriors. The old woman could sense that victory was at hand, but the guns were still firing as warriors, many of them on foot, pushed toward the hill, toward a last group of soldiers.

The old woman was overcome and began to weep, and then she began to sing. Her clear strong voice rose amidst the noise of unfettered violence as she sang a strongheart song, a song of courage and honor for the brave warriors defending their people. She raised her arms in prayer and continued to sing one strongheart song after another while her granddaughter clung to her skirt and watched the battle through wide, fearful, wondering eyes.

Soon the guns stopped shooting and there were shouts of victory. The battle was over and victory belonged to the Lakota and Sahiyela, but the old woman kept singing even as the tears ran down her face. A mounted warrior approached, the strain of combat and the flush of victory on his face. He dismounted and draped a red sash across the old woman's arms. He was a Crazy Dog Warrior, one of an elite group who would often stake themselves in one place during a battle with their red sashes, a visible vow to fight until victory or death. He had seen the old woman, heard her singing, and acknowledged her courage. As he rode away another warrior appeared and did the same, followed by another and another until the old woman was covered with red sashes.

Another old woman told me the story when I was a boy. Woven into her silvery braids were strips of red cloth, cloth given to her by her grandmother. She was the young girl who stood with her grandmother as she sang strongheart songs during the Greasy Grass Fight, also called the Battle of the Little Bighorn, in 1876. Her grandmother had given her the red strips, she said, to remember her by. But the red strips also reminded her that she could be brave. And that's how she faced her blindness every day.

Being brave is having or displaying courage during hardship, being strong in the face of pain. If you don't think you know how to be brave, look around; you'll find someone who does know. Follow him or her. If you follow long enough, you'll learn to have courage, or the courage within you will rise to the top. When that happens, turn around, and don't be surprised if someone is following you.

10

Fortitude

Cantewasake—(can-te-wah-sha-keh)

Strength of heart and mind

✚ The Story of the Old Woman's Dog

Long ago, in the days before we Lakota wandered onto the open grass country west of the Great Muddy River, there was a great summer gathering along a river of many low falls. It was a time of renewal. The Sun Dance had been performed. It was also a time to see old friends and relatives, to learn who had gone on to the next world since the last great gathering.

Many, many people were gathered. There was great feasting, victories were recounted, warriors were honored, and dancing went far into the nights. The camps stretched far along the banks of the River of Low Falls. An arrow from the strongest bow would have to fly ten times to match the length of this great encampment.

Forgets Nothing, a beautiful young woman from a small village of the White Swan band sat at her lodge door preparing porcupine quills to be dyed. She pressed them one at a time against a flat stone with her thumbnail. Not every woman had her patience for this work.

Forgets Nothing could not help but watch the bustle and activity as she worked. Children darted about among the crowds like fork-tailed swallows. Groups of old men sat in the shade of cottonwoods to talk and to trade. Old women had their own groups. Somewhere a drum was pounding softly. She secretly envied the couples who walked by together, for she was not yet married. Not many young men came courting because she had a crooked foot and walked with a limp.

An old, old woman carrying a large bundle and leading a large, handsome dog on a rope broke from the crowds and approached, stopping at Forget Nothing's fire. "All the women want to wear braided porcupine quills in their hair, on their clothes," the old woman said. "Not many want to do the work to turn them into the many colors and braid them. You are young to be doing such fine work."

"I learned this from my mother and grandmother," Forgets Nothing replied. "Sit and rest, Grandmother, if you would like."

The old woman smiled and put down her bundle. She seemed frail, but in her dark eyes there was a light, much like the flickering of a firefly. Her gray hair hung in two braids and her face was etched with the furrows of a long, long life.

"Thank you, Granddaughter. I have passed by many fires, but you are the first to offer rest to an old woman." As yet she had not let go of the rope tied to the dog's neck. Forgets Nothing stood and passed a willow back rest to her guest. The dog lay down as the old woman sat. "This is a fine chair," the old woman said. "It feels good to rest."

"I have tea," offered Forgets Nothing, "and some stew." She noticed the dog was wearing a small, square medicine bundle around his neck. It was decorated with blue quills around the edges. "That is a fine bundle," she observed.

"Thank you. I made it. Thank you also for your kindness. My name is Good Voice," said the old woman. "I arrived only today. I have medicine herbs for some relatives who are not here. So I must go on, though I will return. I have not seen a gathering like this in many summers."

Forgets Nothing served her guest the tea and stew. She was a likable old woman. She ate quietly, savoring the stew as was the habit of old ones. Finished, she returned the large buffalo horn cup and sipped the tea out of a smaller cup. Her clothes were dusty, her moccasins worn. She had traveled far.

"How far must you go, Grandmother?" asked Forgets Nothing.

"Not far," the old woman replied, "but I must show them how to prepare the medicine, so I will be away from here for a few days."

"If you have no place to rest tonight, my mother and I have room in our lodge. Stay with us."

"Thank you. It would be good to sleep on a bed. I have traveled so far. But I must go on now. I wonder if you would help me in another way?"

"I would be glad to, Grandmother," said Forgets Nothing.

"Good," the old woman said. "This is my dog." She stroked the animal's head gently. "His grandmother was a wolf, they tell me. That is why he is so big and strong. He is a very good hunter, the best I have seen. And he is my friend; he listens to me without complaining or talking back disrespectfully. But I took a thorn from his foot only this morning and I want him to rest. Can you keep him here for me until I return? He is quiet and is no trouble."

"I will keep him for you," promised Forgets Nothing. The dog wagged his tail as if he understood. "Does he have a name?"

"Good!" The old woman was happy and labored to her feet. "He has no name. Perhaps you will think of something. I will give you something for keeping him. Remember, he is all I have in the world."

So saying the old woman handed the dog's rope to Forgets Nothing, grabbed her large bundle, and walked away, quickly losing herself in the crowd. Forgets Nothing tied the dog's rope to the smoke flap pole and tossed him a scrap of meat. The dog took it with a wag of his tail, swallowed it, and looked up at Forgets Nothing, his brown eyes bright and inquisitive.

"A name for you is not difficult," she told him. "I shall call you Wolf Eyes, because your grandmother is a wolf. I think you have her eyes."

Forgets Nothing's mother, Corn Woman, returned from a visit. "We have a dog now?" she asked.

"Only for a few days," explained Forgets Nothing. "He belongs to an old woman named Good Voice. He has a hurt foot and she had to travel on, so she asked me to watch him until she returns. I have named him Wolf Eyes." The dog wagged his tail.

"He is a fine looking dog," Corn Woman observed.

As the old woman had promised, the dog was no trouble. He faithfully followed Forgets Nothing through the encampment as she walked about. More people arrived each day and the encampment grew larger. There were many dogs because they were the carriers of burdens, pulling the drag poles piled high with belongings. Except for the very young, all the dogs were big and sturdy, but none were as big as Wolf Eyes.

He stayed next to Forgets Nothing without having to be tied and took as much interest in watching the bustle of activity as she did. She talked to him as she would a good friend, if she'd had one. And he listened with great interest. At night he curled up just beside the door, and there he stayed until the door was opened the next morning.

One afternoon a man with a limp approached Forgets Nothing's lodge and stopped. "My name is Long Walker," he announced. His voice was deep and his eyes flashed; he was dressed well and had the air of a very important man. Forgets Nothing had heard of him. He was a great warrior. "I have passed by and noticed your dog," he said. "He looks strong. He looks like he can pull a heavy load."

"He is a fine dog," returned Forgets Nothing. "And he is big and strong, but I don't know if he has been taught to use the drag poles."

"That is easily done," replied Long Walker. "I have need of such a dog. It has been a moon since I was wounded in a battle. I suffered two arrows in my leg and the wounds have not yet healed, so I need a dog to carry my belongings. What will you take in trade?"

"Oh, I cannot trade this dog to you," Forgets Nothing replied. "He is not my dog. He belongs to an old woman named Good Voice. I am keeping him here until she returns."

"Where has she gone?" he asked impatiently. "Perhaps she will trade with me."

"I do not think so. She told me this dog is all she has in the world. I do not know where she has gone, and I do not know when she will return."

"I have much I can offer in trade," the warrior insisted. "I am a fine hunter with many tanned elk hides to trade. Or perhaps you would like a bear hide robe to keep you warm in the coming winter."

"Those are all good things to trade," the young woman admitted. "But he is not my dog. I cannot trade with you."

Long Walker was losing his patience. "I would wager the old woman who owns the dog would like to have those things, or she is not like any old woman I know. She would be happy to know that you traded such fine things for this one dog. Two tanned elk hides and two bear hide robes!" said the warrior. "That is more than this dog is worth and it is my last offer!"

Forgets Nothing did not like the man's tone, but he was a great warrior and she was only a young woman without a husband. She did not want him to become angrier than he was. "If he was my dog, I would give much thought to your fine offer," she said quietly, "but he is not. I cannot trade him."

"Your stubbornness will get you nowhere in life!" Long Walker spat. Forgets Nothing would long remember the angry flash of his eyes as he turned and hurried away.

That evening she told her mother about the warrior who wanted the dog. "He is well known among all of the bands here," said Corn Woman. "He has two wives and more belong-ings than they can carry. He is a man who gets what he wants. He may return."

That night Forgets Nothing let the dog sleep in the lodge, se-cretly worried that the warrior would take him. But she never saw the man again.

A day later she helped her mother carry some dried meat to the south end of the encampment. A family had given away all of their belongings in honor of a beloved grandmother who had died. Now people were helping them with food and other ne-cessities such as clothing and robes. Wolf Eyes followed Forgets Nothing as if he had always belonged to her and she found her-self growing fond of him. He had an air of calmness and inner strength and people looked at him and not her crooked foot.

The family in mourning had a young child, a girl of eight winters. Her name was In a Hurry because she had been born early. In a Hurry could not keep her eyes away from the dog. Wolf Eyes, of course, was friendly to the girl who had just lost her grandmother. The girl's mother, Leaf, was curious about the dog.

"He is the biggest dog I have ever seen," she said, "but he seems so gentle. Did you raise him?"

"No," replied Forgets Nothing, "he belongs to an old woman. She left him in my care while she visits her family. She will re-turn soon."

"In a Hurry needs a friend," said Leaf. "She was very close to her grandmother. Now she is so lost. She has not smiled since we lost my mother—until today when she saw your dog."

Forgets Nothing was dismayed because she knew what Leaf would ask. "We will stay for a time," she offered. "And I will come again tomorrow so that In a Hurry can play with him."

"My husband and I would be glad to give you what we can for the dog," said Leaf. "Perhaps one of our dogs. My daughter does not take to them at all."

"If he was my dog, I would be happy to give him to your

daughter. I know how it is to lose a grandmother. I was fourteen winters old when mine died. But I told an old woman named Good Voice that I would care for him. Perhaps you can speak with her when she returns."

Leaf was disappointed, but unlike the great warrior Long Walker she was polite. "Perhaps we will come to visit at your lodge tomorrow so my daughter can play with him."

And so they did and visited for the afternoon. Wolf Eyes patiently accepted the friendly attention of the young girl, and she smiled and waved when it was time for her to go home. Forgets Nothing visited at their lodge the following day, but she noticed the wistful look in the girl's eyes when Wolf Eyes had to leave. And so it was that on one day In a Hurry and Leaf would come to visit and on the next Forgets Nothing would take the dog to their lodge. Before long the dog helped the little girl remember how to smile.

Forgets Nothing began to worry that something had happened to the old woman, Good Voice, and because there was no way to know where she was, no inquiries could be made. There was nothing to do but continue waiting for her return. Meanwhile, she found herself growing more attached to the dog.

Early the next morning, when she brought out the night coals from the inside fire pit, she found an old man sitting by the cold ashes of the outside fire pit. Forgets Nothing recognized him. He was Flying By, a very powerful medicine man. His long hair was laced with gray beneath his buffalo horn cap. His face seemed carved from stone, but his voice was low and gentle.

"Granddaughter," he greeted, "I am glad to see you on this fine morning."

"Grandfather," she replied, "I am about to make a fire and will soon have hot tea. Perhaps you will have some."

"Thank you. Hot tea is always good." He laid a handful of twigs near the fire pit and waited as she blew on the coals and dropped dry grass on them. Soon little flames were dancing upward; then she added the twigs.

Forgets Nothing went on with her work as Corn Woman emerged, leading the dog. She recognized the medicine man sitting at her outside fire and was pleased. A visit from such a powerful medicine man could only mean good things. "I am always glad for fine mornings such as this," said Corn Woman. "And my daughter and I are honored to have you with us."

"Thank you, Sister," Flying By replied. "The older I become, the more mornings such as this seem precious."

In a while the tea was ready and Forgets Nothing gave her guest a buffalo horn cup. The medicine man sipped quietly as the women prepared food.They knew he had not come to their lodge for no reason. They were eager to know but waited patiently for him to speak of it.

"I am here to ask something of you," he told them. "This is a fine gathering; many people are here and I have done many sacred ceremonies. There is one I must do some days from now, a ceremony that has not been done for four summers. I am talking of the Thunder Dreamers ceremony."

Forgets Nothing immediately glanced at the dog because she knew about that ceremony. A dog needed to be boiled for it. She said nothing.

"The Thunder Dreamers are very powerful men and important warriors among us. They have asked me to help them with their ceremony. I am here because a dog is a necessary part of what I must do. But the dog that is chosen to be boiled in the pot cannot be any old camp dog. That dog must have certain qualities.

"I have been watching your dog. He is what I need. He is quiet and strong and seems to have a good spirit. As you know, a Thunder Dreamer reaches into the boiling water to pull out the head of the boiled dog, then the other Thunder Dreamers eat the dog's flesh. The dog we kill and use must be a very good dog. If not, the ceremony will be weak and nothing good will be gained. So I have come to ask you for your dog. The Thunder Dreamers need his strength for their ceremony. The gift of such a dog to them would mean good fortune to anyone who gives it." Forgets Nothing was afraid. Flying By was a very powerful man. "Grandfather," she said, sighing, "this is a very good dog. He is very strong and of good spirit. But he is not my dog. I told an old woman I would keep him for her. She is visiting relatives and told me she would return for him. If he were my dog, I would be very honored to give him as a gift to the Thunder Dreamers, but I cannot."

Flying By quietly pondered her words, and his disappointment was plain to see. "Yes," he said, "I can see how it is." He finished his tea and accepted a horn ladle full of buffalo meat soup from Corn Woman. He said nothing as he ate. Forgets Nothing and her mother exchanged nervous looks and waited.

"That is the best soup I have tasted in a very long time," the medicine man said as he gave back the horn ladle. He rose to his feet and smiled. "That is a very fine dog and he is fortunate to have such a good friend. Thank you for your hospitality." The old man turned and walked away without a backward glance.

In a Hurry came that afternoon to visit, and as she sat playing with the dog a small figure emerged from the crowds and stopped. It was Good Voice. Forgets Nothing was never so happy to see anyone in her life. "Grandmother," she said, "it is very good to see you. I hope your journey was good."

The old woman put down her bundle and sat. "All journeys are good," she replied. "We learn something from each one, good or bad. It is good to see you also, and to know that you have taken good care of my dog." She looked at the young girl next to the dog. "And you are on a sad journey. I can see from the ashes on your cheeks that you are mourning."

"Yes," said Forgets Nothing, "In a Hurry has lost her grandmother."

Sorrow and compassion washed over the old woman's face. "Grandmothers are the very best friends anyone can have. There is no way to replace them," she said, reaching into her bundle and pulling out a small ball of fur. It was a puppy. "Sometimes we can try to find new friends. I found this one along the trail, but I am afraid she needs someone young to run and play with. I cannot do that. Can you help me?" she asked In a Hurry. "She needs a friend like you."

The girl's smile was as bright as a new rising sun as she took the puppy in her arms. "How can we pay you?" Leaf asked.

Good Voice smiled at the girl. "Never forget your grand-mother," she advised. "Payment is not needed."

The smile on the girl's face would not go away as she and her mother departed with the puppy.

"Grandmother," said Forgets Nothing, "that was a very kind thing, for you to give a puppy to that little girl. It is fortunate that you found a puppy on your journey."

"Life provides the gifts if we know where to look," replied the old woman.

"I am glad you have returned and that your journey was good," said Forgets Nothing. "Your dog—I call him Wolf Eyes— is so big and strong that some want to have him."

"I know," replied the old woman. "I thank you for keeping him. Elk hides, buffalo robes, and good fortune are very fine things to have. Many would have traded the dog. A great war-rior, a heartbroken girl, and a powerful holy man all have strong need of the dog. But you have a strength of mind; you honored your promise to me. I am grateful."

"How is it that you know?" Forgets Nothing was astonished.

"It only matters that I know. I also know that few people have your strength of mind. Others would have traded the dog for the fine things that were offered and then told me that the dog wandered away. Life will reward you for that."

From her bundle she took a long wooden vial and gave it to Forgets Nothing. "For your foot," she said. "Rub it on every day. It is a salve made from the ankle bones of the pronghorn antelope. As we know, they are the fastest runners on the flat-lands. Their ankles are thin but very, very strong."

Good Voice stayed the night in the lodge of Forgets Nothing and Corn Woman. Forgets Nothing awoke at dawn and was not surprised to see the old woman's bed empty. The dog, too, was gone. She spent the day going about her chores with a feeling of emptiness. That evening she rubbed the salve on her ankle before she went to sleep.

More empty days passed. She missed the dog and his inquisitive stare, but she also missed the old woman, especially when she noticed that the stiffness in her ankle seemed not as bad.

One evening Forgets Nothing went to watch the dancing but stood at the outside edge of the dancing circle, envying all who could dance. She kept to the shadows, as she always did, because she did not want people to see that she walked with a limp. Like a sudden cold rain a feeling of loneliness fell upon her as she watched several couples do the long, winding Snake Dance side by side, hand in hand. The drums pounded like a heartbeat, like the soft rhythm of life itself. Forgets Nothing saw couples who had eyes only for each other as they danced—and felt herself outside the flow and the rhythm.

"Grandmother," she said, talking to Good Voice in her mind, "perhaps I should have asked if you had a husband for me in your bundle." In a moment she turned away from the dancing and walked slowly back to her own lodge.

She was at her fire outside the lodge the next morning when a figure stopped before her, blocking the low rays of the morning sun. "I have just arrived," said a low, deep voice. "I will gladly give you all this meat if you would cook but one meal for me."

Forgets Nothing shaded her eyes to look at the stranger. He was tall with inquisitive eyes. His shoulders were wide and on his drag poles was the carcass of a freshly killed deer.

"If you cut up the meat, I will cook it for you," she replied.

The man went to work. Forgets Nothing could see he was not much older than she, and his face was strong and pleasant. She built up her fire as Corn Woman emerged from the lodge.

"Mother," she said, "we have fresh meat. This young man was kind enough to bring it."

The young man stood to acknowledge Corn Woman, and Forgets Nothing gasped as she noticed a small bundle tied around his neck. Its edges were quilled in blue.

Soon the smell of roasting meat floated about as Forgets Nothing carefully tended her cooking. The young man finished cutting up the meat and hung the pieces on the racks next to the lodge. Now and then Forgets Nothing glanced at the bundle around his neck. It was exactly like the one around the neck of the old woman's dog.

"I will go to the river and wash," said the young man.

"When you return the meat will be ready," replied Forgets Nothing. She noticed he walked with a slight limp. He had neatly laid aside the drag poles next to his weapons and his large bundle.

"He does not yet have a wife," observed Corn Woman, to which Forgets Nothing could only stay silent, but her heart was pounding.

Before long he returned and a skewer of meat was waiting for him. He sat and politely waited.

"Have you an injury?" asked Forgets Nothing. "You are limping a little."

"It is nothing, only a thorn through the sole of my foot," he replied. "Someone removed it for me."

"Have you come far?"

"Yes," he said, "I have been traveling for many, many days. I have never been here, to this part of the country, so I was lost."

"Where are you going?"

"Wherever life takes me," he answered, smiling. "You have many questions."

"Yes," said Forgets Nothing, "and I have another. Who are your people and what is your name?"

He smiled again. "I believe I am from the White Wolf band. My parents were killed when I was very young, and so I was taken and raised by my aunts and several grandmothers. I have a name, but I do not remember how it was given to me. My name is Wolf Eyes. What is yours?"

Walking on Grandmother's Road

Grandmothers in every Native American culture, and no less among us Lakota, are the epitome of all the virtues we strive to learn and practice. One virtue they epitomize best of all is fortitude. At a powwow in the 1970s I sat behind my paternal grandmother and another of my grandmothers, Nancy White Horse. I was engrossed in their conversation about grandchildren and their stories of the people who had passed on since the last powwow. Grandma Nancy noticed I was listening and beckoned for me to lean closer. For reasons unclear to me at that moment, she said, "If you want to go far in life, walk Grandmother's Road."

Fortitude is Grandmother's Road. I know now that if we Lakota had not walked Grandmother's Road, that moment with those two grandmothers at the powwow would not have been possible.

The demise of the bison—*tatanka*—and the overwhelming encroachment of Euro-Americans were the two primary factors that ended our free-roaming life as nomadic hunters. The bison were decimated purposely and the onslaught of Euro-Americans could not be stopped. Consequently, a lifestyle hundreds, if not thousands, of years old came to an end almost overnight. We found ourselves confined to reservations where we not only had geographic limitations to contend with but also an intensive effort to tear our culture away from us. We were to become farmers—learn the "virtues of hard labor" and turn into "productive citizens." In the process, our spiritual beliefs were ridiculed and reviled.

The new ways were not easy and though a few of us did sincerely embrace them and change, most of us were reluctant. We could not resist militarily so the only viable option was to go through the motions and make the best of the situation. We had to find a way to resist that would not bring repercussions. The only option was to walk Grandmother's Road.

Historians, sociologists, and anthropologists look at the period between 1890 and 1940 as merely a time of change. From the viewpoint of the government, the savage Lakota had been tamed and a concentrated effort was underway to civilize him. No one, as far as I know, took a close look at the emotional and societal effects of change within the Lakota community. If anyone had, it would have been discovered that women were in the forefront of a new order.

Traditionally women were the focal point of family, the comforters and nurturers around whom family life revolved. That role didn't change: Instead it became even more critical. Women didn't usurp the male's role as head of the family; they were too wise to take away the only responsibility men had left. During one of the most difficult periods in Lakota history, women fulfilled their ancient societal role and saved their culture. They held their families together in spite of the sad fact that children were taken away to boarding schools. A woman who was taken as a very young child to a missionary boarding school remembers lamenting to her mother that no one was permitted to speak Lakota. The dormitory matrons had sharp ears and were quick to severely punish any child caught breaking the rules. The woman's mother gave a bit of simple advice that symbolized an undercurrent of quiet resistance. "Whisper," she said.

If the objectives of the government and the missionaries had been realized, we Lakota would be totally converted to Christianity, speaking only English and regularly denouncing our former "heathen" way of life and more than likely singing the praises of Euro-Americans for rescuing us from ourselves. The fact that we still exist culturally has its basis in the quiet fortitude of many of our grandparents and great-grandparents.

Instead of overtly resisting, they quietly, but stubbornly, hung on to their ways. When their children came home from the boarding schools wearing short hair and speaking English, they hid their heartbreak. When the government outlawed the Sun Dance, the faithful simply danced where no one could see them. When the priests and ministers harangued them for their misbegotten ways, they smiled and nodded, went to a church on Sunday, and then convened at a sweat lodge on Wednesday. They learned to speak English and told the old stories in their second language because they knew their pride was not as important as keeping the stories alive. In short, they used the last weapon available to them in order to save the essence of being Lakota: fortitude. Two generations of Lakota walked Grandmother's Road. The ultimate result will be that the traumatic changes in lifestyle and all the losses suffered in the past 150 years will one day amount to nothing more than a bump in the road.

Fortitude is quiet strength, closely related, obviously, to bravery and perseverance. Along with bravery, generosity, and wisdom, it is considered one of the four greatest virtues. Grandma Nancy White Horse's accurate name Grandmother's Road reminds me of the particularly hard winter of 1951–52. My maternal grandparents and I were living in a log house three miles from the nearest highway and seven miles from the nearest town. There were at least two heavy blizzards that lasted for two or three days. One of those storms was particularly strong. The mournful howl of the wind only added to the tension I felt and I'm sure my apprehension was obvious to both of my grandparents. If either of them was worried, it certainly wasn't detectable in their behavior. They went about their daily routines without a single comment about the cold, the wind, or the snow piling up outside. I vividly recall my Grandma Annie beading a leather bag. In fact, she had me string beads for her while she told me childhood stories of my mother and uncle. Her calm voice and demeanor were reassuring and the storm became inconsequential.

A few years later I recall walking along a river bottom with my grandfather when a sudden wind sprang up. He pointed to a grove of sandbar willow along the river and we watched how they bent with the wind. Not far from us we heard a loud crack as an oak tree lost a branch. Sandbar willows are slender and about five to six feet tall. They grow in thick stands along creeks and rivers. We watched as they bent with the wind and lost leaves to its sharp gusts, but none of them broke. The oak, with its obvious strength, didn't withstand the wind as well. Fortitude is like the sandbar willow. To have that kind of strength we must learn to bend with the wind.

I was living with Grandmother Blanche Marshall in 1979 and was with her the night she received the news that her oldest son had died accidentally. I listened as her son-in-law, my uncle by marriage, gently and respectfully broke the news to her. Grandma Blanche sat with her hands folded in her lap listening just as respectfully, occasionally wiping away a tear. In the days following she was the picture of quiet, dignified strength. On the day of the funeral she was the last to stop at the open casket. Only then, as she embraced her son, did she weep and give voice to her grief. Somehow she managed to do even that with a dignity that seems particularly inherent in Native-American women, especially the grandmothers.

Fortitude is what gets you through the moment your teenage daughter announces she's found a special on belly-button piercing (and then turns into Attila the Hun when you say no). Fortitude helps you endure the shock and disappointment of not getting the raise and promotion you were counting on. Fortitude helps you live from one minute to the next when you learn that your precious child is missing in action in some distant land or port of call. Fortitude comes to your rescue when you're suddenly faced with the unexpected. It is, I believe, quiet persistence, the ability to take one step at a time and make the best possible use of your attributes, which may include a quick wit, quiet confidence, a deep faith, or simple endurance, among others.

Long ago there was a race among all the animals on the Plains. Each of the large animals had boasted that he was the best. The bison touted his great strength. The antelope bragged of his great speed, as did the hawk and the falcon. Not to be outdone, the deer said he was the swiftest. The wolf, the fox, and the coyote insisted they shouldn't be overlooked. Of course, with each one convinced that he was the best, there was no way to know the truth of it.

So the animals held a great council and it was decided that a race was the only way to settle the question once and for all time. Each tribe of animals was to select its very best for the race, which would consist of four laps around the *Paha Sapa,* the Black Hills. Every tribe sent its very best and the prairie around the Black Hills was crowded as the animals gathered. Every tribe on the Plains was represented, from the bison to the mouse— one of every kind of four-legged, of every kind of winged, and of every kind of crawler. It was quite an impressive sight.

The racers gathered at dawn and as the sun rose over the eastern horizon they were off. As one would expect, the antelope left everyone behind followed closely by the falcon and the hawk. Up near the front were the bison, the deer, the bear, and the great cat. A noise like thunder rose up over the mountains as the race wore on and a great dust cloud followed the racers. On and on they went, a great mass of bodies running, and flying, and crawling as fast as they could. By the time the first circle of the Black Hills had been completed, those who had started out so swiftly had fallen behind. Now leading was the wolf, followed by the great cat, the fox, the hare, the swallow, and the owl. And everyone else was not far behind.

Somewhere during the second circuit many animals began to stumble and everyone was sweating badly. As the third lap around the mountains began, the wolf was still in the lead and the bison, the antelope, and the deer were far, far back but still determined to win. In fact, no one yet thought he could lose. A strange thing happened then: some of them began to sweat blood, but still they kept running, and flying, and crawling.

The final circle of the Black Hills began with the wolf still in the lead, but now behind him was a flock of birds, among them the swallow, the owl, the meadowlark, and the magpie. The great throng of animals was lagging behind now, many of them barely moving and all of them trying so hard that many more were sweating blood. As the finish approached, the wolf looked back and saw no one, but above him he heard a strange, flapping sound: It was the magpie.

Now the magpie is not the most graceful of flyers; in fact, he is the only bird that looks clumsy in the air. But there he was, flapping along. The wolf began to fade—even his great endurance was waning—and ever so slowly the black and white magpie pulled ahead to win the race. No one had ever thought this clumsy bird had a chance.

To this day every animal pauses to look up as the magpie flaps by in acknowledgment of his victory. And to this day the Earth around the Black Hills is red with the blood of the racers.

◇◇◇

Lorenzo Stars, a quiet, soft-spoken young man, had a dream, but there were many obstacles. His family was by no means wealthy. In fact, his father, who had farmed for many years, died prematurely of a heart attack. Lorenzo pursued his dream anyway, working to earn money and finding scholarships. Sometimes the money ran short and he had to take time off from school to work, but always he went back. He never, for one moment, let go of his dream. His road through medical school was a little longer than usual, but now he is Dr. Lorenzo Stars. At the moment he is temporarily assigned to the Wagner, South Dakota, Indian Health Service Clinic. Before that he was at the Rosebud Indian Health Service Hospital, on the Rosebud Sioux

Indian Reservation. Dr. Stars is an enrolled member of the Rose-bud Sioux Tribe.

We all want to be strong all of the time; we want to enter the race at our best; we want to be swift and graceful and embody all the attributes the world seems to reward most. But in the real world we are not all strong; we are not all swift; and we can't face every circumstance with every attribute or resource we should. But whatever we have or don't have, whatever we are or aren't, no matter how tired or disillusioned we are, there is still a need to be met—an objective to be reached, a dream to be realized. Chances are we won't reach our objective in one giant step. Success is rarely the result of one fell swoop, but more often the culmination of many, many small victories. Dr. Stars didn't achieve his dream in one momentous act; he made it happen with a series of accomplishments, each placing him one step closer to his goal. We Lakota still have a strong culture because our parents, grandparents, and great-grandparents persisted in quiet little ways, thereby preserving the essence of who and what we are through the same fortitude that brought victory to the magpie.

My maternal grandparents planted a vegetable garden every summer until the early 1950s. Grandpa Albert plowed with a single bottom plow pulled by two big draft horses. The garden was always labor intensive. In addition to planting, cultivating, and weeding, we had to haul water to the garden and water by hand from buckets. But the result was always worth all the work. Every fall we harvested enough corn, potatoes, squash, beans, and pumpkins to get us through the winter—and there were luscious watermelons in summer. One fall we had a thinner harvest, and not because we didn't work hard enough to care for the garden. It was mid-July; the corn was taller than I was and we were doing our usual tedious chore of picking bugs off the potato leaves when my grandfather spotted something just over the western horizon—a thin, black cloud. Without stopping to explain why he instructed me to pile dry kindling and green grass at several spots around the garden. I followed his lead, as did my grandmother. All the while they kept an eye on the black cloud heading in our direction.

As each pile of kindling was built my grandfather would light it, and as soon as it was burning high enough, he would add green grass to create thick, white smoke. I was puzzled at first, but while neither of my grandparents had time to stop and explain, I knew it had something to do with the approaching black cloud. Very quickly we had managed to make a thick, white smudge over the garden. Then I heard a buzzing noise as the black cloud was directly overhead and I was horrified to find myself inside a swirl of grasshoppers. My grandfather handed me a wet burlap bag and shouted, "Kill them!"

My grandmother kept the smudge piles burning while Grandpa and I fought the grasshoppers. Fortunately, the bulk of them kept flying east, but enough of them descended on our garden to do considerable damage. I swung that burlap bag until my arms were ready to drop off. In spite of the many grasshoppers I knocked down, hundreds more still crawled everywhere in our garden. It seemed as though every leaf were covered. We knocked so many down that they crunched beneath our feet, but we didn't stop. By sundown we seemed to be winning, but by then every leaf in the garden had been eaten to some extent. After the sun went down we lit lanterns and torches and kept working. Around midnight Grandpa declared that we had probably saved most of the garden. The next day we raked up dead grasshoppers and burned them.

We had lost about half our garden to the grasshoppers. Weeks of work and patient care were obliterated in a few short hours. Yet neither of my grandparents complained about our sudden misfortune. "Sometimes this happens," they said. Our harvest was smaller that year but I learned again that fortitude does have its rewards.

Grandmother's Road is not difficult to find. It is connected to all the other roads in life, perhaps because victory does not always go to the strongest or the swiftest. Those who turn onto Grandmother's Road will find there is no room for impatience or despair, for those who use it do not necessarily move swiftly. Grandmother's Road will, however, more often lead to victory than any other route.

11

Generosity

Canteyuke (chan-te-you-keh)

To give, to share, to have a heart

 ## The Story of Brings the Deer

Sometimes it's easy to forget that we live in a place, this world, where many other beings live, too. As two-leggeds, humans, we believe we are the most powerful beings to walk the Earth. We don't seem to understand that the power that comes from being numerous is not the same as the power that comes from being wise, or kind.

Long, long ago, it is said that our people lived in the cold north country. No one knows for how long, but they had to find a new place to live because there came several winters of near starvation. The snows were very, very deep and the great curved-horn deer, the caribou, which they hunted for food, seemed to have gone elsewhere to live. Only a few were found and they were old and sick and their meat was tough and stringy. Finally the people noticed that the wolves were gone, and they knew they had more than likely moved to some other place where the deer were plentiful. That winter was very hard. The meat from the few old and sick deer had to be given out in small portions, and many old people died because they gave their meat to the very young.

The council of old men talked and talked about the difficulty that was a visitor in their lodges and decided it would be wise to do as the wolves had done. It was time to find a new place to live and perhaps when the deer returned, they could return as well.

In the spring, after the snows began to melt, those that were still alive made preparations and set out toward the south. There were many forests to the south, they had heard, and perhaps there was deer to be found there.

Day after day for many, many days they traveled and it was not long before they had eaten all of the food they carried with them. It took all the skills of their hunters to find rabbits and squirrels enough to feed everyone. A sudden spring blizzard came upon them, but they were able to pitch their small lodges in the shelter of a forest and hide from the icy breath of the north wind and the sting of the flying snow. The blizzard howled for days and there was nothing to be done but huddle inside the lodges and wait. Finally there came a dawn that was silent and very cold. The people emerged from their small lodges to see that a new blanket of snow covered the land from horizon to horizon. There was a great silence, also, and it seemed that they were the only beings on the face of the Earth.

The old men advised everyone to gather wood and build fires while they talked among themselves. Staying warm was necessary, of course, and the people knew how to warm themselves in winter. The greater worry was their empty food containers. If something more than a few rabbits and squirrels could not be found, they would starve. The old men had a plan.

All the men were sent into the forest to find as many rabbits and squirrels as they could. They were able to gather enough meat to last several days. Then the old men revealed their plan. Two of their best young hunters were to be sent deep into the forest to find deer. All the squirrel and rabbit meat was dried and prepared for them. That night the two hunters who had been selected prepared their weapons and made ready for their journey.

As the new dawn broke the two hunters tied on snowshoes and headed into the forest. This was new country to them; they didn't know the land as they had in their old home. They paused often to look at their back trail so that they could find their way back to their people.

The forest was thick and dark, but many of the trees were not unknown to them, especially the *wazi,* a pine that grew thick and tall. As yet they had seen no animals except for squirrels and rabbits, and they had found no tracks. They wondered what kind of animals they would see in this new country. The one they didn't want to meet was the great white bear, who was the most powerful and fiercest of all the four-leggeds. It took many hunters with long lances to kill one white bear.

They ate their dried meat only a little at a time and when a squirrel or a rabbit was close enough for good shot, one of them would kill it with an arrow so they could have a little fresh meat. If there was a miss, the arrow was lost in the deep snow, and arrows could not be wasted. An arrow lost meant one less chance. They were mindful of such things because they knew that the hopes of their people walked with them and they were determined to be successful. And so each morning they prayed for strength, skill, and courage. And each day they faced the cold and the uncertainty as they moved deeper and deeper into the forest.

After many days of travel they saw tracks that looked like deer, but they were small. The great curved-horn deer of the north had large, wide split hooves. The tracks they found were those of small split hooves. Still, they were encouraged and followed the tracks.

Many days on the trail had weakened them and even though

they had been very careful, their food bag was nearly empty. They awoke one morning to a cold wind that made it difficult to light a fire, but worse than that it wiped out the tracks they had been following. There was nothing to be done but wait out the wind. The next dawn was again cold, but it was clear and calm, so they set out once more. To remain strong enough to face the cold and the deep snow they had to eat, but unless they found fresh meat soon they would not have the strength to finish their hunt.

They found no tracks the next day and the forest was strangely silent. That night as they rested and warmed themselves by their fire the two hunters spoke of what to do.

"Our relatives are waiting and they are hungry," said Sees the Bear. "We must go on."

"Yes," agreed Left Hand, "but we should return to the meadow where we saw the tracks, and we must hunt until we find something or until we no longer have the strength to walk."

They found the meadow the next day and a few tracks the snow had not covered, but walking through the deep snow on snowshoes had sapped their strength. And what the snow didn't take from them the cold did. They made camp and ate the last of their food.

By sunset of the next day all they had was a fire to keep the cold away, and it barely did that. They had no food. The next day was the same. They had found no tracks of any animal, and each day thereafter they could feel their strength leaving them a little at a time. After that they began to stumble often and soon they couldn't travel long without stopping to rest.

It was the afternoon and they had managed to build a fire as they rested. Left Hand had fallen into a snow-filled gully and it had taken all of Sees the Bear's strength to help him out. Both hunters shivered as they sat sadly staring into the flames. Suddenly there was a crashing through the trees and a form dashed past them and into that same gully. It was a deer, a kind they had never seen before, with a gray coat and great forked antlers. It fell into the gully onto its back and struggled mightily to turn over.

The hunters couldn't believe what they saw. "Your bow!" shouted Sees the Bear. "We must shoot it quickly!"

They moved as swiftly as they could, but the cold had numbed their fingers and they had difficulty placing their arrows on the strings of their bows. The great gray deer had gained its feet and was nearly out of the gully before they could shoot. But two arrows flew straight and the deer was mortally wounded. With a last great leap he flew over the gully's rim, then fell in a heap, never to move again.

That night the hunters feasted on the deer's heart and their strength returned. The next day they made drag poles on which to load the carcass and pull it through the snow. It was a very large deer, but it had small, cloven hooves and there was much meat that they would save for those who waited.

They began their return journey strengthened by their success. Not knowing what to expect, they took turns guarding the deer at night. It was on the second night of the return journey that Sees the Bear thought he was having a dream. As he sat by the fire huddled beneath his robe, a skinny coyote appeared in the firelight and spoke.

"It has been a hard winter," Coyote said, "and my family is hungry. If you are a kind being, you will give us some of your deer meat. We would need only a little to get us by."

Sees the Bear rubbed his eyes, but the coyote was still there, sitting just at the edge of the firelight. He woke Left Hand. "I think I am having a strange dream. Look there and tell me what you see," he said.

Left Hand looked around and saw the coyote. "A coyote," he said. "I have never seen one this close to a fire before."

"You are great hunters and I know you have good hearts," said the coyote. Left Hand was astonished. "I am an old woman and have lived a long life, but it is for my family that I beg your kindness. We need only a little of your meat," she said.

Left Hand laughed. "We are having the same strange dream because I heard that coyote ask for our meat."

"It is not a dream," realized Sees the Bear. "Look how thin she is, and she is old."

"We cannot help her," sniffed Left Hand. "We must take this meat home to our relatives. They are hungry, too!"

"We cannot let her and her family starve," said Sees the Bear. "The spirits were kind to us by sending this great deer. We can share a little of it."

So saying he sliced off a strip from the hind quarter and tossed it to the coyote. "Listen at night and my family will sing our gratefulness," Coyote said as she took the meat and disappeared into the darkness.

"That was a foolish thing to do," said Left Hand.

Two days later as the hunters rested at midday a flock of magpies alighted in the branches around them. "We are hungry," one of them said.

"It is winter!" Left Hand replied angrily. "Winter is a time of hunger! Our people wait for this meat that we have killed. They are very hungry!"

"The wolves took the insides of the deer you left behind," said the head magpie. "They left us a little, but it was only a very little. We are hungry."

Before Left Hand could stop him, Sees the Bear cut several thin strips of meat and tossed them to the magpies. Cawing loudly they swooped from the trees and took the meat. "You are kind," said the head magpie. "We will repay you. Hereafter, if you do not see us or hear us, it will be a sign of hard times. If there is to be plenty, we will come and announce it." Then the magpies were gone as quickly as they had come.

"That was a foolish thing to do," said Left Hand.

The traveled as far as they could each day, of course, making camp as the sun went down and then starting again as the dawn broke. Dragging the deer on the poles across deep snow was not easy, but they knew their relatives were waiting. And who knew if they had found anything to eat while the hunters were away?

As they stopped briefly to rest, a gray, shadowy form approached through the trees. It was a large wolf and he had a badly injured foot. The hunters were wary; they had never seen a wolf so close.

"If you are here to ask for meat, we cannot give any more!" shouted Left Hand.

"I am sad to hear you," said the wolf. "As you can see, I have hurt my foot and although I have been able to find the deer, I cannot chase them. My wife has given birth and I must take her fresh meat so that she can suckle the young ones."

"Our story is sad as well," replied Left Hand. "Our people are starving; they have not eaten for many, many days."

"Yes," said the wolf, "the winter has been hard for all of us, and I thought there may be kindness in your hearts."

"There is," said Sees the Bear. "We have just enough to share." In spite of Left Hand's protests he sliced off a chunk of meat and tossed it to the wolf.

"I am grateful," said Wolf. "For your kindness you shall have my skill as a hunter."

Left Hand was angry. "See what you have done?" he shouted. "You have given away most of our meat! What will we tell our people? They sent us out because we are the best hunters. We are fortunate that this deer fell into that gully full of snow. If he had not, we would be freezing to death somewhere. Yet you have given meat to every beggar who has come to you!"

"I will tell them the truth," replied Sees the Bear. "The old ones have taught us that it is good to share. Is that not the truth?"

"No more!" shouted Left Hand. "There is barely enough to feed our people now!"

They traveled in silence thereafter with Left Hand hanging on to his anger. They made camp in the shelter of an old riverbank. "I think we are one more day's walk from our lodges," Sees the Bear said.

Left Hand gathered firewood and kept his silence.

It was a fox who came next, that night while Sees the Bear was on watch and Left Hand was sleeping. "I have never seen such a hard winter," he said. "The snow is so deep it is difficult for me with my small feet. The rabbit can run on top of the snow while I sink in. I wonder if you would be so kind as to give me some of your meat."

Sees the Bear glanced at Left Hand sleeping soundly beneath his robe, remembering the younger man's anger. "Yes," he whispered to the fox, "I think there is enough to share." Thereupon he sliced off some succulent ribs and gave them to the fox.

"I am grateful," said Fox. "My people are very skilled at hiding. For your kindness that skill shall be yours."

In the morning, of course, Left Hand could see immediately that more of the deer was gone, and his anger burst like the sudden flight of the prairie grouse. "I cannot travel with you any longer!" he said. "You have given away most of the meat! What will we give to our people?"

"There is enough," insisted Sees the Bear.

"There is not enough for us all!" shouted Left Hand. "I am returning to our lodges alone, ahead of you. I must tell our old men what you have done! See that you do not give away any more of our food! I will bring some young men to help carry what is left!"

True to his word Left Hand departed angrily. Sees the Bear was left to struggle with the deer. Traveling on the ice of frozen streams he was able to make some progress, but it was still very difficult to drag the deer by himself. The first night alone he was so exhausted he built a snow cave and slept without a fire. As he was preparing to travel the next morning he came across a hawk with an injured wing.

"What has happened to you?" asked Sees the Bear.

The hawk flashed his great yellow eyes. "I fought with the short-tailed cat. He attacked me after I had caught a rabbit. Now I cannot fly until my wing is strong again. I have not eaten in many, many days."

Sees the Bear gave the hawk a chunk of deer meat. He hung it up in a tree so the hawk could be safe, away from other hunters.

"I am grateful," said the hawk. "I have not seen your kind of people here."

"We have come from the north," said Sees the Bear. "The winters were very hard and the great curved-horn deer moved away. To keep from starving we had to move also. After traveling for many, many days we came to a forest and pitched our lodges. We were out of food, so our people sent two of us out to hunt. We hunted until our food ran out and then we killed this deer. He had trapped himself in deep snow."

"Follow this forest until you come to the lake country," advised the hawk. "The hunting there is very good; the forests are filled with large and small deer. When the snows melt, you can catch fish from the lakes."

"Thank you," said Sees the Bear. "My people will be glad to hear that news."

That afternoon he reached his people's lodges. He hid what was left of the deer in an old hollow tree and entered the camp. The old men, the leaders, were waiting for him. "Left Hand has told us what has happened," he was told. "Now it is for you to speak for your side of the story."

Sees the Bear did not hold back the truth and told everything as it happened. "We have brought back meat," he said, "and I think it will make us strong enough to travel south. The hawk told me that the hunting in the lake country is very good."

"Some food is better than nothing," one of the old men said. "And if your friend the hawk tells the truth, we can build our new homes in the lake country."

Sees the Bear felt very sad to see the disappointed faces of his people. There would be food enough to go around, but there would have been more if he had not given much of it away. With his head hanging down he led the men to where the meat was hidden.

"In that hollow tree," he said. "It is there."

Left Hand was the first in and he grabbed the deer's leg and pulled. It was very heavy so he asked for help. Finally four young men had to pull the deer out of the tree. To everyone's great surprise the deer was whole.

"This cannot be!" cried Left Hand. "There was barely half when I left him yesterday. I cannot understand this!"

As the men stood around looking at the carcass of the gray deer, there appeared a ghostly white form of a great deer with very large forked antlers. The men backed away in fear.

"I am the deer who live in the forest," said the Great White Deer. "There are many of us and our flesh will give you strength. We ask in return that you always show your gratefulness for the gift of our life. If you do this, we will always be here to help you. Generosity is a good thing to have for we are all travelers together on this Earth."

The Great White Deer disappeared into the forest. The men returned to the camp with the deer and that night there was a great feast. Somehow there was more than enough meat to go around and some to save as well.

Sees the Bear was honored and he was given the new name of Brings the Deer. After he had rested, he hunted again and returned with another deer. And as the Great White Deer had asked, he paused at the body of the dead gray deer and spoke a word of thanksgiving.

The people were strengthened and were anxious to travel. When the warm spring winds melted the last snows, they broke camp and went south. There they found the land of plenty the hawk had described to the man whose name was now Brings the Deer.

Brings the Deer became the most skillful hunter the people had ever seen. It seemed as though he had powers and abilities that no other man had, and through his life he always seemed to know when hard times lay ahead. He was seen to toss scraps of meat to the magpies that came around the village; soon all the people did likewise. And it was said of him that he would smile whenever the coyotes sang their evening songs.

Left Hand had a difficult life. He was nearly killed by a bear one summer and almost drowned while trying to spear fish. More than that, strange things seemed to happen to him more often than to anyone else. Once a great wind came with a rain storm and the only lodge in the village blown over was his. Many wondered quietly why it was that his bows broke quite often during a hunt. Perhaps it was because of the difficulties that visited his life that Left Hand didn't smile very often.

Many men hunted with Brings the Deer and many brought their sons to him so that they could learn his skills. There was a small ritual that he taught everyone: Each time a deer was killed in the hunt, he would pause for a quiet moment and then he would lay down a bundle of sage as an offering. To this day there are still Lakota hunters who pause to speak a word of thanksgiving for the gift of the life of a deer.

From the Earth and from the Heart

If Lakota societal values seemed to discourage the accumulation of material possessions, it was also true that generosity was encouraged and exemplified. Paraphrasing an ancient sentiment helps us understand why generosity is necessary: "The Earth Mother gives us all that she has. We must do the same." Generosity, therefore, is a timeless virtue that lives in the heart. Indeed, the literal translation of the Lakota word for generosity, *canteyuke,* means "has a heart."

One of the sacred ceremonies of the Pipe brought to us and taught by the White Buffalo Calf Maiden is the *Hunka,* which means "to forever move." The Earth tells us, "I shall forever be, or move as, your mother." We are given assurance that no matter how good or how bad we are, no matter how happy or miserable, because we are children of the Earth she will always love us and provide for us. Therefore, our concept and practice of generosity comes from the Earth itself.

Our stories tell us that the White Buffalo Calf Maiden came to us a few thousand years ago, so as far as we're concerned we've been around awhile. And in that time, though we have experienced change, life did not ever change as swiftly and with as much difficulty as it has in the past 300 years, and especially in the past 150 years. Prior to the sudden changes experienced by the past three or four generations, we lived a primitive lifestyle.

As with any human society anywhere we had the basic needs of food, shelter, clothing, and security. We provided for those needs by hunting and gathering. In the bigger picture our lifestyle was dictated by the environment around us. In other words, our ancestors didn't make an arbitrary decision to be hunter-gatherers. They had to function as such because it was the best and most logical method of survival.

Like most of the peoples who lived on the prairie, our ancestors were nomadic. Camps or villages were moved primarily to accommodate the activities of hunting and gathering. Our primary food resource was the bison, a migratory herd animal, although it also provided materials for shelter and a variety of other necessities as well. We also hunted other large game—the deer, for example—and smaller game such as rabbits. We gathered various food and medicinal plants in season; among them were wild oats, prairie turnips, peppermint, apples, plums, and a variety of berries. Obviously, our livelihood was derived directly from the Earth, in keeping with her promise. Because she was so generous with us, we had to demonstrate the same generosity in our relationships with all living things. The Earth shared with us and taught us to share.

One of the most enriching customs still practiced on every

Lakota reservation is the Giveaway. It is simply that; stuff is given away in celebration, in observance, or in memoriam.

We Lakota need only the slightest reason to get together to feast or dance, or both. Every summer there are powwows on every reservation and in urban communities where there is more than one Indian. We eat and we dance and we have a good time. But there is more to it than that. We are sharing. We share the food, the dances, and the good times.

Rarely is there a powwow where some special ceremony is not performed, usually a traditional name-giving, the honoring of someone's accomplishment, the honoring of a veteran or veterans, or a memorial. Whatever the special ceremony, it is done very publicly. For example, a family will bestow a traditional Lakota name on a child, and anyone who wishes can watch and then join in the dancing to honor the recipient of the new name. Then the child's family does the Giveaway. In appreciation for everyone's attention, participation, and good wishes, boxes, bags, and baskets full of stuff are given away. Stuff can be anything from candy bars to horses. The usual Giveaway items are star quilts, blankets, sheets, scarves, pillow cases, towels, wash cloths, soap, silverware, clocks, watches, costume jewelry, shawls, sunglasses, Thermos jugs, pens, and so on. At the conclusion of the Giveaway, at least one person, though frequently several, publicly expresses appreciation for the excellent gifts received and commends the family for a fine ceremony. And then there is more dancing.

Giveaways are an especially significant part of memorials. A memorial is a gathering and a feast usually a year after a death to honor the deceased person. It is in keeping with the Releasing the Spirit ceremony brought to us by the White Buffalo Calf Maiden. This observance allows the family and the community to reconcile with the death and enables the spirit of the deceased to make the transition to the Spirit World. There is always a feast where the family of the deceased serves those in attendance. Prayers are offered and a revered elder known for his or her wisdom counsels about life and death. The occasion is concluded with a Giveaway.

The Giveaway as a significant part of many occasions, observations, and ceremonies is so much more than the obvious. It is a mechanism for sharing. The giving of material gifts symbolizes the giving away, the sharing of joy, honor, or sorrow. When the gift is accepted, the recipient also accepts the joy, the honor, or the burden of sorrow.

Generosity should not be limited to humans, however. All living things are related because we are all children of the Earth. And everything we do affects the Earth and everything on it, including the human race. The more water we pollute, the less there is for us to drink. The more land we contaminate, the less we have to grow crops. The more forests we cut down, the less oxygen there is for us to breathe. We humans have made the Earth needy by our greed and selfishness, both rooted in the idea that the Earth was created for us. Nothing could be further from the truth. We are of the Earth. The Earth has promised to care for and provide for us no matter who or what we are. We must understand that we are stewards of the land and as such we have a sacred responsibility to all our relatives to seriously and thoughtfully live up to it. This responsibility is to the present generation as well as those yet to come.

As a species we humans have come far because of the generosity of the Earth. She has given us a home as well as the means to raise ourselves to lofty heights, if only in our own minds. It is far past the time to repay her with our generosity.

We Lakota believe there are many roads in life, but that there are two that are most important: the Red Road and the Black Road. They represent the two perspectives to every situation, the two sides of every person, the two choices we frequently face in life. The Red Road is the good way, the good side, and the right choice. It is a narrow road fraught with dangers and obstacles and is extremely difficult to travel. The Black Road is the bad way, the bad side, the wrong choice. It is wide and very easy to travel. The Red Road and the Black Road appear in many of our stories, not as roads but as the personifications of right and wrong, good and bad, light and dark. The two hunters in "The Story of Brings the Deer" are an example. One hunter is not generous, he doesn't want to share; the other is most generous and gladly sees to the needs of others.

Consider the ultimate fate of each hunter. Left Hand, who was not inclined to share, was frequently faced with negative consequences and had a hard life. Brings the Deer is generous, almost to a fault, but he is rewarded with the skills and abilities of those he helped. Generosity has its rewards. The Earth Mother appears as the Great White Deer and asks for nothing more than a simple acknowledgment of the gift of life. One must pause and consider the human species and wonder which hunter we have been. Furthermore, how have we acknowledged the gift of life from the Earth?

Generosity has its rewards. The lack of it has consequences.

In the past the accumulation of material goods among the Lakota was not unknown. But it wasn't done in the pursuit of wealth; it was done as a hedge against hard times and to help anyone who ran short. Still, it wasn't practical for a nomadic people to accumulate too much because it only meant more to haul when the camp was moved, which was at least two or three times a year. The more you owned, the more you had to haul.

A certain man had many possessions because he was reluctant to part with anything he owned. His dwelling was filled with all manner of things and he had a large herd of horses to carry it all each time the village moved. Though he had all those fine things, he had no friends, and he was getting old and didn't want to spend his last days alone.

He sensed that his time was drawing near and he wanted the people to think and speak well of him after he died. So he spoke to the wisest old woman in the village. "What is the answer?" he asked. "I do not want to spend my last days alone."

"Be generous," the old woman replied.

The old man pondered the woman's advice and then sent the camp crier among the people to announce that he would make a feast and that everyone was invited. The day of the feast came and the people gathered. True to his word the old man fed all the people. Then he gave away all of his possessions, all of his horses, and even his lodge. He left himself with only the clothes he wore—no lodge to sleep in and no horse to ride—but that night he was invited to sleep in someone's lodge, and the next night in another lodge.

And so it was until the old man died. He had no possessions, but he had many friends, and it was spoken of him that he was a generous man.

12

Wisdom

Woksape (wo-ksa-peh)

To understand what is right and true, to use knowledge wisely

✛ The Story of the Man Who Spoke Softly

In a certain village there was a leader, a headman, who was respected for his quiet ways and good decisions. He did not ask to be a leader, but as a young man he had shown that he could think clearly and act calmly on the battlefield. And he was a good provider for his family and took care of the helpless ones. The people liked those ways and so they asked him to be a leader. This was, of course, in the old days. Today, in these times, men want to be leaders for the power and the glory of it, and not always because they have the good of the people truly in their hearts.

So the man reluctantly became a leader, and over the years he made good decisions and always spoke the truth in the village council meetings, whether the truth hurt or helped. So for many, many years under his leadership the village prospered and was strong.

Two generations grew up under his leadership, and the headman was getting on in years. A few young men of his village yearned for a new leader. They talked among themselves and decided it was time the chief's blanket was passed to another, a younger man with more daring, more dash and flair befitting the reputation of a prosperous and powerful village. They had forgotten who had helped to give their village that reputation.

A few of the young men met secretly and formed a plan they were certain could not fail. They would catch a small bird, approach the old headman, and ask him a question. "Grandfather," one of them would ask, "I have a bird in my hand. You are wise. Is the bird dead or alive?"

If the old headman answered, "Alive," the bird would be crushed. If he said "Dead," the bird would be released to fly away. Either way, the old headman would seem to be weak and uncertain, and the people would doubt his ability to lead.

So on the morning of an important village gathering the young men caught a sparrow, and one of them was chosen to approach the old headman. In the afternoon when all the people had gathered, the chosen one approached, calling out in a loud voice so that all the people would hear.

"Grandfather, I have an important question to ask you," he shouted. A hush fell over the entire gathering as the young man approached the old headman, holding something behind his back.

"Grandfather, I have a bird in my hand," the young man said as all the people gathered around. "Since you are wise, is the bird dead or alive?"

The people waited, for many of them knew that some of the young men were yearning for a change in leadership. A few of them wondered if the young men might be right. Perhaps it might be time for a younger man to assume leadership. So they waited for the old headman to respond.

The old headman approached the young man with the question. He stood quietly for a time, seeming to study the ground. Whispers went through the crowd. Was this finally the challenge that would be too much for the old headman?

The headman turned to the young man and smiled patiently.

Then he spoke firmly but gently as he always did when something important was before the people.

"Grandson," he said, "the answer is in *your* hands."

✛ The Story of the Woman Who Gossiped

In the village was a woman who liked to gossip. She never told anything that wasn't true, but she did make certain that everyone in the village knew every little secret that fell on her ears. And, of course, she always expressed her opinions about what was wrong or what should have been done.

One day the woman who gossiped overheard a young couple's argument, and soon after the husband went hunting and didn't return for nearly a month. The gossip was quick to let everyone know what was happening in the lives of that young couple. Then she suggested that the young husband had left because his wife would no longer welcome him under her sleeping robes. So they would never have children.

The young wife heard the whispers and was deeply shamed and embarrassed. Her shame was so strong that she ran away and her brother trailed her for many days before he found her and brought her home.

Thereafter the people of the village spurned the gossip, turning their backs whenever she approached. Eventually no on spoke to her at all. After that her husband left her and returned to his own family's village, and the gossip was the loneliest person in the village.

Not knowing what to do, she finally took her troubles to the oldest woman in the village, one who was known for her wisdom and kindness.

"Grandmother," asked the gossip, "what must I do so that people will talk to me again?"

The old woman handed the gossip a handful of white down

feathers. "Take these feathers and place one at the door of every person you have gossiped about. Then come back to me."

The gossip did as she was told and returned to the old woman without a single feather.

"Now," said the old wise woman, "go back and gather the feathers you have placed at every doorway and bring them to me."

The gossip began to weep. "I cannot, Grandmother, for you see, the wind has taken them all and they are scattered. I cannot bring them back."

"Yes," said the old woman, "they are like the hurtful words you have spoken for so long. You can never bring them back; even so you chased after them all of your life. There is only one thing you can do: Never say such hurtful words again. But first take a gift to everyone you have hurt and shamed with your words as a sign that you will change your ways."

The gossip took the old woman's advice. She had gossiped for so long that she gave away everything she owned, except for one dress. Thereafter she was known as One Dress, but when it was clear that she had changed her ways, the people forgave her. One Dress lived a long life and was known as the woman with the quiet ways.

A Lesson from the Gully

An old Lakota man and his eleven-year-old grandson walked across the deep snow of the northern Plains one winter in the Moon of Popping Trees. They were returning from a hunt carrying four large jackrabbits.

The boy was cold and hungry and eager to be home in the small but cozy log house he shared with his grandparents.

"Grandpa," he said, "can we take the shortcut through the gully with the spring? If we do, we will be home sooner. I know

Grandma must be worried about us because it will be dark soon."

"That is a summer shortcut," replied the old man. "This has been a hard winter. I have not seen this much snow in many years. That gully is sure to be filled with snow, and it will be too deep for us to cross."

"How do you know that?" the boy asked. "We have not been near that gully since the first snows."

"True," answered the old man patiently, "but every winter when there has been deep snow that gully has been filled. No one, not even the coyotes, dares to cross it."

"The rabbits do," the boy pointed out resolutely.

"They have large, flat hind feet. They can stay on top of the snow," explained the old man.

"How deep can it be?" the boy wondered. "My legs are long. I can cross that gully."

The boy hurried on ahead, leaving his grandfather behind. He called out as he went, "I'll boil you a pot of coffee before you get home."

The old man watched the boy head for the shortcut. He followed in the tracks the boy left, stopping only to pull a long rope from the burlap bag he carried. Then at a certain place he turned for the end of the gully, to the right of the boy's path.

Near the end of the gully the old man trudged to a windswept rise nearly bare of snow. There he stopped, reached once more into his burlap bag, and took out a flat stone with a hole in the middle. He threaded the rope through the hole and tied it securely.

Shading his eyes, he studied the snow-filled gully below him, finding a long snowbank extending halfway to the opposite hillside. At the head of the snowbank the boy's tracks ended at a large hole in the snow's crust. The old man smiled.

Gauging the distance to the end of the snowbank, he grabbed the stone with the rope tied to it and swung his arm back and forth two or three times. After the third time he tossed the stone up. It arched, then bounced on the top of the crust of snow. The old man retrieved the stone by pulling on the rope and tried again. This time he tossed the stone higher. It arched again and hit the snow, breaking through the crust. Then it sank down through the soft snow underneath.

The old man grasped the end of the rope and called out.

"There is a rope in the snow; if you grab it and hold on, I will pull you out."

Nothing happened; the rope remained slack. The old man waited a moment and called out again.

"Grandson, there is a rope in the snow. If you grab it and hold on, I will pull you out. Now it is your pride that is keeping you from taking the rope. Soon it will be the cold. Your fingers will be too numb to hold on."

The old man waited. Soon the rope tightened and he began to pull, anchoring himself in the snow as he did. He tugged and tugged. The weight of an eleven-year-old boy in the snow is not easy to move. Soon, however, the snow-covered head and shoulders of the boy broke through the crust and he struggled to his feet.

The old man brushed the snow off his grandson as the boy stood hanging his head.

"Do not feel bad, Grandson," the old man said lovingly.

In a moment the boy spoke, even as he shivered from the cold. "Grandpa, how did you know I was under the snow? Are you wise?'

"Yes," the old man answered, "I suppose I am wise."

"How did you become wise?" the boy wanted to know.

"First," the old man said, "I learned all I could, and so I know many things. I know about trails, about winters, and about eager boys who think they know something. Everything that I know came from the Earth and everything on it, in it, beneath it, and above it. Also I have lived a long life."

"That is being wise, Grandpa?"

"No," the old man went on. "That is knowledge. Being wise,

having wisdom, is knowing what to do with what you know, when to do it, and how to do it. Or, sometimes, a person must know enough to do nothing."

"What do you mean," the boy wondered.

"I knew you would try the shortcut no matter what I said," the old man pointed out.

"Why did you not stop me?" the boy asked, still shivering.

"Because wisdom told me that you had to learn the lesson for yourself," the old man said. "Because wisdom reminded me that I learned the same lesson in the same way. My grandfather pulled me out of the same gully."

The boy smiled. "You fell through the snow as I did?"

"Yes," said the old man, "and that was the day I started my journey, the journey toward wisdom. Just as you have now. Remember what happened here when it comes time to pull your grandson from this gully when it is filled with snow."

Life's Gift

There was a time when I wondered why old people were so wise. I don't anymore because now I know that wisdom is life's gift. Life demands that we exercise perseverance, face adversity with courage, demonstrate fortitude in the midst of temptation, tell the truth no matter how painful, walk in humility, sacrifice for our families, practice generosity to be truly rich, respect all who are part of the Great Circle of Life, choose honor above personal gain, act with compassion toward the needy, strive for harmony in personal relationships, and otherwise demonstrate the virtues that give meaning to life. And even if we don't succeed most or even some of the time, life rewards us for trying—for living: It grants us wisdom.

What is wisdom? Is it knowledge? Knowledge is the basis for wisdom, but it is not a guarantee that wisdom will follow. Wisdom is knowing what to do and say, or what not to do or say. A grandmother, for example, watches a child about to play with the fire, as all children do from time to time. As curiosity draws the child closer and closer to the fire, the grandmother hovers closer to ensure that no harm occurs but as yet has not issued a warning of danger. Then the inevitable occurs. The child pokes a finger in the flames and yanks it back, away from the pain of the heat. Then the grandmother says, "Grandson, the fire is hot, it can hurt you." Her words affirm a fact that is indelibly etched in the boy's awareness. He will at least think twice before poking a finger in the flames again, and there is a high probability that he will never again deliberately touch fire. If she had spoken the words before the occurrence, they would have held no meaning for the child, and they would not have prevented him from touching the flames. Her knowledge of the situation came from her own childhood, when she did the same. After a lifetime of acquiring knowledge and experience, she knew the most effective moment to affirm the truth. Wisdom also told her that, in this case, it was better to demonstrate the truth rather than simply explain it.

Wisdom is the antidote for impatience, willfulness, exuberance, anger, ignorance, arrogance, and a host of other tendencies that invariably place us in harm's way, set us up for embarrassment, or cause us to hurt others. Wisdom can prevent us from making fools of ourselves and enable us to leave a lasting, positive impact. It is the sum of the experiences—the highs and lows, the good and the bad, the successes and failures—that are a part of our life's journey. Wisdom comes from the light as well as from the darkness; it gives us depth of insight, the perception that only comes from experiencing our numerous struggles.

When I was five I watched my grandfather build a log house practically on his own. I was eager to help but managed to be underfoot more than anything. He never scolded me for misplacing his tools at a critical moment when he needed a wood rasp or for pounding nails in the window frame he was about to fit into the log wall. And he found a way to use my enthusiasm to keep me out of his and harm's way. He was peeling logs—removing the bark from dried logs—before lifting and fitting them into their places in the wall. Grabbing an ax, he swung it and sank the blade into one end of a log, then asked me to keep the handle of the ax vertical. It would keep the log from rolling and help it dry, he said, as long as the log didn't move. I grabbed the handle of the ax and made absolutely certain that the log stayed perfectly still. With a periodic inquiry as to how my chore was proceeding, while ensuring that I remained safely out of the way, my grandfather was able to finish a critical phase of the building process and build my self-esteem as well. To this day I truly feel I helped him build that house.

During an especially hard winter, after that log house was finished, my grandmother settled my fear of the howling blizzard wind. She calmly performed her chores, totally unaffected by the white chaos just outside the windows. She asked me to stack the firewood next to the cookstove in a particular order, in a crisscross pattern where one layer of split wood, four across, pointed opposite to the layer underneath. As I concentrated on piling the wood correctly, I forgot about the howling wind. Later she asked for my help as she beaded a leather bag. First she had me count out so many red beads, then so many white, and so on; then, I was asked to thread them on a long string for her. This chore, too, took my mind off the storm. As the day wore on and I'd become engrossed in the stories she told and the various chores that were invaluable to her, I noticed that the wind had died down. She taught me that the wind was not the most fearful thing, but that the fear itself was and to cope with it first was the best way to handle adversity.

There comes a time in our lives when we can't run as fast or walk as far; our reflexes slow down, our hair turns gray or silver, and the roads we have traveled begin to appear on our faces. At that point we will have come to the most critical and most rewarding phase of our lives: We have a life we can look back on, not because it's ending but because we have walked far and that journey is now our reward and our strength. We have acquired wisdom. Wisdom is life's gift to us, but it is also our gift to life.

We remember people for their accomplishments, sometimes for a single achievement or for their character. Years of public service, winning a Nobel Prize, twenty-five years as a political prisoner, the number of home runs in a single season, a hole in one at Pebble Beach, or a lifetime of selfless service to the poor will live long in our memories. If we choose, there are numerous examples in the world for us to remember and emulate. Yet in moments of introspection or when a crisis weighs heavily on me, I tend to think of those people with whom I had or have a close association: parents, grandparents, teachers, or friends. Those are the people I turn to because I know them, and I remember them for their wisdom.

It is told that when a man was asked what virtue he wanted to be known for, his answer was honor. When all is said and done, I would prefer to be known for my wisdom. I would like to be remembered as one who reciprocated life's gift.

Afterword

Wicoiye Ihanke

The People

My earliest recollections are of hearing Lakota spoken by my parents and grandparents. The first stories I heard were of Lakota people, of exciting and fascinating events that gave substance, dimension, and affirmation to everyone around me: my Lakota parents, grandparents, and relatives. There was no other way for me to be or think in those childhood years. Looking back on that time, I understand that the innocence of childhood told me I was living in a Lakota world.

The Lakota were and are part of the largest indigenous nation on the northern Plains of North America. The other two-thirds of the alliance are the Dakota and the Nakota, located east of the Missouri River in what is now South Dakota. The Lakota are west of the Missouri.

The three words—*Lakota, Dakota,* and *Nakota*—have the same meaning, "an alliance of friends." They represent geographic as well as linguistic distinctions. Numerous strong linguistic similarities between the two eastern groups suggest that they were one group several hundred years ago, and there are enough differences between the two eastern dialects and Lakota to suggest that there were two different languages at one time: one spoken by the Dakota and Nakota and another spoken by the Lakota. This was, of course, before the three names were coined. It is likely that those two separate groups met, formed an alliance, and over time evolved one language with three separate dialects.

We know that the three groups, as one nation, were in the Great Lakes area until the late 1600s. The Ojibway (a.k.a. the Chippewa and Ashinabe), who had a more convivial economic relationship with the French, acquired firearms and drove us west. As a matter of fact, because of the Ojibway we are probably better known to the world as the Sioux.

The Ojibway called us *naddewasioux,* which probably means "little snakes" or "little enemies." The French, probably their voyageurs, shortened the word to Sioux. The word has a significant place in the contemporary names by which we are known: Rosebud Sioux, Cheyenne River Sioux, Standing Rock Sioux, and so on.

The Dakota are composed of four subgroups, and the Nakota have two. My direct ancestors, the Lakota, are composed of seven subgroups, often called *Oceti Sakowin,* which is "The Seven Fires" or "The Seven Council Fires." Those subgroups and the meanings of their names, as well as any contemporary designations, are

Oglala—to scatter; Pine Ridge Sioux,
Sicangu—burnt thigh; Rosebud Sioux, Lower Brule Sioux,
Hunkpapa—those who camp on the end; Standing Rock Sioux,
Mniconju—those who plant by the water; Cheyenne River Sioux,
Oohenunpa—two boilings or two kettles,
Itazipacola—without bows, and
Sihasapa—black feet, black soles.

As the allied people moved west from the Great Lakes, the Dakota settled in the area that is now roughly southwestern Minnesota, northeastern South Dakota, and southeastern North Dakota. (The names for those two states are taken from the Dakota dialect of our language.) The Nakota established a territory that encompassed southeastern South Dakota and a small portion of northeastern Nebraska. Both groups apparently found the climate and topography east of the Missouri River quite conducive to their semisedentary, agrarian lifestyles. The Lakota, meanwhile, pushed west across the Missouri onto the open prairies. In fact, they became known to the eastern groups as *titunwan oyate,* which means "the people of the open" or "dwellers on the prairie."

Lakota territory eventually stretched west from the Missouri River to the Big Horn Mountains and north from the North Platte River to the Yellowstone River. In our language those landmarks are, respectively, *Mnisose* (the Great Muddy River), *He Wiyakpa* (the Shining Mountains), *Pankeska Wakpa* (the Shell River), and *Hehaka Wakpa* (the Elk River).

My ancestors had lived a woodlands lifestyle in the Great Lakes area, more than likely for several generations. On the open prairies of the northern Plains they returned to the nomadic hunting lifestyle they had probably known earlier. Euro-American historians are quick to say that the arrival of the horse around 1680 was the turning point that changed the semisedentary Lakota into nomads. My ancestors were nomadic hunters before the arrival of the horse. The horse only enhanced an already established lifestyle.

My mother's Lakota people are *Sicangu,* which means "burnt thigh." A small, extended family group of Lakota people was traveling (on foot because they didn't yet have horses) across the prairie in late summer, more than likely to relocate their camp. A prairie fire, probably started by lightning and whipped by the winds, raced across the grasslands. The travelers attempted to outrun the flames without success, so they made a fateful decision. Running back through the fire, they decided, was the best course of action under the circumstances. And so they did. There were injuries, of course, and some deaths. Some of the very young and very old were overcome by the heat and smoke, but most of the people survived. Many of them suffered terrible burns, especially on their upper legs, on their thighs. Thereafter they called themselves the Burnt Thigh People.

From my mother's side I am a Burnt Thigh, or Sicangu. From my father's side I am Oglala.

The horse fit in perfectly with the nomadic lifestyle. The logical and eventual consequences were an expansion of territory, larger dwellings (horses could carry much bigger loads than dogs), and larger families. By the mid 1800s we were probably about fifteen thousand strong, the largest group on the northern Plains. We developed a more exciting way to hunt the bison, of course, and evolved into some of the finest light cavalry in the world. We were a horse nation and proud of it. Consider the song of a Lakota warrior to his war horse:

> *My friend, my brother,*
> *Carry me forth when the sun rises,*
> *Let my courage be as great as yours,*
> *Let us move like the wind*
> *To defend the helpless ones.*
> *We shall go forth as one*
> *To meet that which awaits.*
> *Should I see the sun set tomorrow*
> *It shall be your victory,*
> *And I will sing songs of you*
> *And you shall wear ribbons of red.*

In fact, we and other tribes of the Plains were so readily identified with our horses that a white observer was compelled to comment, "Every Indian male has six legs, two of his own and four belonging to his horse. He does everything from his horse and gets down only to dance or to die, and would probably prefer to do both on horseback."

Horses became so much a part of Lakota lifestyle that each family owned at least a few, some more than others, of course. There evolved a system of specialized use, though most of a family's horses were used for basic transportation or for hauling household goods. Everyone learned to ride at an early age.

Horses were so valuable they became a medium of trade, but their greatest value was as war mounts and buffalo-hunting horses. Each was a distinctly separate discipline and specific traits were sought for each use. War horses needed a calm disposition in addition to speed and endurance, and were trained to do specific tasks, such as dragging his rider away from harm when he was unhorsed in battle. Buffalo hunters had to have breakaway speed and were taught to overcome their inherent fear of buffalo. Both kinds of horses were given years of training until they could respond to their riders' cues—primarily leg pressure and weight shift—without the aid of a rein of any kind. Thus it was not uncommon for a buffalo-hunting horse to take his rider to a specific buffalo, maintaining a close distance to give his rider the opportunity for a bow shot, while both were racing at about thirty miles an hour.

Horses enhanced the Lakota lifestyle and became an inseparable part of our identity. Without them we would not have been able to resist the encroachment of Euro-Americans for as long as we did. Without them our history would have been drastically different.

◇◇◇

A cornerstone of Lakota culture can be summed up in the words family and kinship. Family is the backbone, the foundation of our culture. We are given substance, nurtured, and sustained by family. Kinship goes beyond family and is the connection we feel to the world at large and everything in it.

Given the concept of family, it isn't difficult to understand the idea of kinship with other forms of life—*everything* was of the Earth. We all came from it one way or another and returned to it when life was over. These were the unalterable realities that connected us to everything around us.

A phrase essential to and used in all of our ceremonies is *mitakuye oyasin,* which means "all my relatives." Its definition reminds us of that connection. Many of our stories about animals refer to them as "the elk people," or "the bear people," or "the bird people" not because we were anthropomorphizing them but because in our language the designation "people" was not limited to humans. This kinship, this sense of connection, also served to remind us of our place in the great scheme of life. We were not the fastest or the strongest of creatures, but we had the ability to reason that enabled us to survive the same way that a bear's strength, an antelope's speed, or an eagle's keen eyesight sustained existence. And like many of our fellow beings, we lived by hunting.

We became nomadic hunters because there was no choice. If the bison wasn't one of the reasons we migrated onto the Plains, it quickly became the focal point of our survival. The bison was the greatest nomad on the Plains and our association with and dependence on it turned us into nomads as well. As the bison went, so did we.

There were moments when my ancestors felt invincible, especially as they watched the great numberless herds of bison. There were millions and millions of them and only a few thousand of us. Because we had learned to be wise enough to take only what we needed, those herds seemed like an endless supply. We were the largest tribe on the northern Plains, and we were pushing against the foothills of the Rocky Mountains by the time we began to have consistent contact with the newcomer who would change our lives.

By the early to mid 1700s the Sicangu Lakota were in what is now south central South Dakota, having established a roughly triangular territory, the base of which dipped down into the current north central Nebraska. In 1803 the first organized exploration led by Lewis and Clark skirted the eastern edge of that territory as they went north. In the late 1820s and early 1830s a group of French explorers made their way through our territory as well and buried an inscribed lead plate on a hill near what is now the capital of the state, Pierre. In 1837 we—as well as the Mandan far to the north of us—experienced a foreshadowing of things to come.

By the 1830s the Euro-Americans had navigated almost the entire length of the Missouri River with their steamboats, and established several landings. In early summer of 1837 a steamboat from St. Louis traveled north on the river and stopped several times. One of its stops was at what is now southern South Dakota, at the Whetstone landing, near the present town of Pickstown. Another, and the last, was at Fort Union in what is now North Dakota. Trade goods, including blankets, and a few travelers were off-loaded at both stops, along with the small pox virus carried by the travelers or the goods, or both. By the end of that summer about two thousand Lakota, as well as a like number of Mandans who lived in earth lodges near Fort Union, had died from smallpox. That summer's epidemics would not be the last on the northern Plains, but we learned that there were consequences from contact with the newcomers.

The first whites had come alone or in small groups, but that changed in the late 1840s. Then began a twenty-year migration that would bring hundreds of thousands of whites across the southern end of Lakota territory—not only hundreds of thousands of people but their horses, mules, oxen, wagons, and household goods. They also brought more disease and an arrogant mindset that the lands across which their two-thousand-mile trail stretched were empty and available for the taking. The Oregon Trail began in western Missouri, went across northeastern Kansas, southern Nebraska, southeastern Wyoming, southern Idaho, and on into northeastern Oregon, ending at

Portland. In western Nebraska and southeastern Wyoming the trail crossed Lakota territory.

The migration interrupted the flow of life on the Plains, altering the migration patterns of animals, especially the bison. The land along the corridor of the trail was dotted with the graves of the thousands of emigrants who lost their lives to accidents, starvation, and sickness. Household goods such as beds, trunks, stoves, tables, and so on were discarded and left. And animal carcasses were left to rot where they died.

The white emigrants were afraid of attack from the tribes who lived along the trail, and that fear resulted in the first of several treaty negotiations at a place in southeastern Wyoming known to us as Horse Creek, and to the whites as Fort Laramie. Our fears regarding the emigrant travel were disease and the possibility that some of the travelers might decide to take up permanent residence on our lands. Both fears were realized, of course. Surprisingly, the first contacts we had with the emigrants were friendly, or at least there was no outright conflict. We were curious about them, obviously, and we traded with them. But that would change all too soon.

The United States peace commissioners with whom we treated at Fort Laramie assured us that the emigrants were just passing through and would need no more space than the width of their wagon wheels. Then they told us it would be in our best interests not to attack them. There were essentially no armed clashes until the U.S. Army attacked us first, because of a cow.

A Mormon traveling along the trail in 1854 lost or turned loose a cow. It was a pitiful animal, from all reports, nothing but a walking bag of bones. The cow wandered into a Sicangu Lakota camp and was shortly dispatched and butchered by a visiting Mniconju Lakota. Unfortunately, the Mormon wanted his cow back. The headman of the village, a wise old man named Conquering Bear, spoke his regrets and offered a horse in trade. The Mormon wanted nothing but his cow, so Conquering Bear increased his peace offering to several horses. All to no avail. Negotiations broke down at that point and a young Army lieutenant named Grattan was sent to the camp to straighten out the matter. His idea of settling the issue was to bring a mountain howitzer with thirty soldiers and open fire. He and twenty-nine of his soldiers were killed in a brief but savage skirmish. Among the casualties on the Lakota side was the beloved headman Conquering Bear. A boy of fourteen happened to be visiting relatives in the camp and he witnessed how the Army had tried to handle the situation. That one incident would stay with him the rest of his life. The boy's name was Curly or Lighthaired Boy. As a young man he was given the name Crazy Horse.

The Army retaliated and about a year later attacked another Sicangu Lakota camp, under the leadership of Little Thunder, while many of the men were away hunting. The soldiers commanded by General Harney wiped out the entire camp—to teach us a lesson, they said.

Conflict came among us and stayed thereafter. We fought to protect ourselves and from that difficult era emerged many of our heroes: Little Thunder, Conquering Bear, Red Cloud, Crazy Horse, Gall, Sitting Bull, Spotted Tail, Big Foot, and a host of other leaders lesser known to Euro-Americans, but no less revered by us. All shared a common dream to preserve the Lakota way of life and all of them dedicated their lives to it. Many did lay down their lives.

Several significant events from 1855 to 1890 shaped our destiny, two of which were the Fort Laramie Treaty of 1868 and the discovery of gold in the Black Hills in 1874. The treaty established the entire western half of what is now the state of South Dakota as the Great Sioux Reservation, in perpetuity. In addition, we could hunt in what was called unceded territory encompassing parts of western North Dakota, eastern Wyoming, and northwest Nebraska. It was an arrangement that was workable, but six short years later the treaty was seriously compromised by the discovery of gold in the Black Hills. Prospectors and miners poured into the Hills in direct violation of the treaty, adding to the already steady stream of whites into Lakota territory. United States peace commissioners were dispatched to negotiate for the Black Hills, which resulted in the Agreement of 1875. That "agreement" sliced off the western third of the Great Sioux Reservation, which, of course, included the Black Hills. Some stories suggest that the peace commissioners and the army's representatives coerced older Lakota leaders, past their prime and influence, to sign the agreement by threatening to transport their people to Oklahoma Territory in the middle of winter.

The die had been cast and many Lakota leaders realized that the only course left was to resist militarily. One of those leaders was Sitting Bull of the Hunkpapa Lakota. In the spring of 1876 he sent messengers to other leaders and called for a gathering in the summer. Fully one-fourth of the Lakota nation responded and by the time of the summer solstice, six thousand to eight thousand were encamped, first near Ash Creek and then by the Greasy Grass River. That river was also known as the Little Bighorn.

There were many battles in the thirty-five-year period from 1855 to 1890. We fought because we had no choice. Some of the battles have long since been forgotten, but a few have caught the world's attention. The Battle of the Little Bighorn in 1876—where the Oglala Lakota Crazy Horse and the Hunkpapa Lakota Gall, two noted battle leaders, led just over a thousand fighting men—handed the U.S. Army's Seventh Cavalry the worst defeat ever suffered by the army in the West. It is also know as Custer's Last Stand. Eight days prior, Crazy Horse, with a force of seven hundred to nine hundred Lakota and Northern Cheyenne, had fought General Crook to a standstill at the Battle of the Rosebud. Ten years earlier a younger Crazy Horse had been instrumental in the defeat of the soldiers from Fort Phil Kearny at the Battle of the Hundred in the Hand: the Fetterman Massacre according to the history books.

Long before the arrival of the whites my ancestors had developed a concept and practice of warfare based on the demonstration of courage rather than killing an enemy. It was more honorable and far more courageous, they thought, to touch a live enemy in battle than it was to kill him. Warriors were killed in battle now and then, but killing was not the first and foremost intent. Other tribes had similar philosophies, and sometimes pitched battles were fought in which only a few men were wounded; whichever side demonstrated more daring, skill, and courage was the victor. This approach to warfare was set aside once the Lakota began in earnest to resist the whites militarily. In our estimation they didn't understand our sense of honor, but they did understand killing. Several historians and writers have stated that the great warrior Crazy Horse emulated the fighting tactics of the white soldiers because their way was superior. That was not the case. Crazy Horse was one of the first to point out that the only way to defeat the whites was to kill them—because that was their way.

The Battle of the Little Bighorn was a turning point for us. Though we had been victors in a significant battle, it was as though we had awakened a sleeping giant. The United States government responded to that embarrassing defeat with relentless pursuit, even to the point of attacking in the winter. Soon after the Little Bighorn, a Cheyenne force was caught and defeated at the Battle of War Bonnet Creek in northwestern Nebraska. Later that same year American Horse's band was defeated at the Battle of Slim Buttes in northwestern South Dakota, and Crazy Horse's camp was attacked, demonstrating that no one was safe from the army. Sitting Bull, meanwhile, fled to Canada hoping to find sanctuary there, but confusion among some of his younger leaders caused dissention and he eventually returned, in 1881. After a stint with Buffalo Bill's Wild West Show, he settled down on the Standing Rock Reservation.

One other significant factor that determined the course of events from 1876 to 1890, perhaps even more important than the discovery of gold in the Black Hills, was the wholesale slaughter of the bison. The once seemingly endless resource numbering in the millions was whittled down to a few thousand, no longer adequate to support the free-roaming nomadic lifestyle for several thousand Lakota. General William Tecumseh Sherman, the proponent and practitioner of "complete warfare" during the Civil War, applied the same strategy in dealing with the Lakota. Primarily due to his encouragement, hundreds of white buffalo hunters slaughtered bison by the thousands, if not hundreds of thousands across the Plains. Sportsmen were encouraged to come out West and do their part in taming the wild Indians by killing off their lifeline. It was not an uncommon sight for trains to roll through bison country with dozens of rifles shooting out both sides of passenger cars. By 1900 there were probably less than fifty bison south of the forty-eighth parallel, or the border between Canada and the United States. Without the bison my ancestors lost a literal and figurative source of strength.

In May of 1877, Crazy Horse and his followers were the last to surrender to the inevitable by turning themselves over to U.S. authority at Fort Robinson, Nebraska. Crazy Horse had been promised his own agency, or a reservation, where his people could learn to adjust to their new way of life. The army, however, was leery, suspicious that Crazy Horse would lead an uprising and renew hostilities. Unfortunately, jealousy among his own kind fomented rumors believed by the army commanders that led to his untimely death. When informed by a Crazy Horse detractor that he was at the head of a plot to kill General Crook, the commanding officer at Fort Robinson issued orders for his arrest and incarceration. On September 5, 1877, while resisting arrest, Crazy Horse was stabbed by a soldier with a bayonet. He died shortly after midnight and with him died, for all intents and purposes, the will to resist.

The final chapter of Lakota resistance was the Ghost Dance. After the death of Crazy Horse the Lakota gave in to reservation life. A series of "agreements" with the United States continued to slice up the Great Sioux Reservation little by little, eventually resulting in several smaller reservations amounting to a small fraction of the original land base. The environmental, spatial, and psychological adjustments for that first generation of Lakota were traumatic. Guns and many of their horses were taken away and they were expected to learn how to farm. Missionaries waded in realizing that a defeated people were ripe for conversion. In 1887 the United States Congress passed the Dawes (or Homestead) Act, which only served to further reduce Indian land holdings. That act ended treaty making with all Indian tribes and introduced individual land ownership to Indians. A census was taken and the reservation lands were surveyed, then land was allocated to males eighteen years of age and older. Those with families were given 160 acres and single men 80 acres. Thereafter the leftover surplus lands were opened up for homesteading by whites. It was as if the Great Sioux Reservation never really existed.

In 1888 a Paiute Indian from Nevada had a vision during an eclipse of the sun and began to preach the Ghost Dance religion. The Earth would be returned to the condition it was in before the coming of the whites if all Indians learned to live together harmoniously and shun the ways of the whites, he said. They also had to pray and meditate and perform a dance in which they would briefly die and then glimpse the life to come, complete with bison and their dead ancestors. This message of hope took hold among the Lakota and some went to the Southwest to learn more about it.

The message of hope was given a new twist among the Lakota: The performance of the Ghost Dance would eliminate the whites. Ghost Dance shirts were made and many people believed they had the power to stop bullets.

After the Ghost Dance caught on with a fervor, the nervous federal government sent troops in among the Sicangu and

Oglala, fearing that a military uprising was in the making. Perhaps the Ghost Dance would have phased out over time, but the presence of troops only fueled the embers of resistance still smoldering in many Lakota. The Indian agent on the Standing Rock was especially nervous that Sitting Bull would join the movement, and on December 15, 1890, he sent a detachment of Indian police to prevent the still influential leader from becoming involved. Sitting Bull resisted arrest, however, and he and seven of his men—including one of his sons—were killed.

Meanwhile, Big Foot's Mniconju Lakota band of 350, mostly women and children living along the Cheyenne River in north central South Dakota, had fled southward, having been invited to the Pine Ridge reservation by Red Cloud and other reservation leaders who were hoping to help restore calm to the situation. The United States Seventh Cavalry—the same unit that had been so shamefully defeated at the Little Bighorn fourteen years earlier—caught them thirty miles east of the Pine Ridge agency on December twenty-eighth. Along with the Seventh was the Ninth Cavalry, the famed Negro unit known as the Buffalo Soldiers. They escorted Big Foot and his column to Wounded Knee Creek and ordered them to encamp for the night. That night and the next morning soldiers searched for weapons and found only broken and inoperable pistols and rifles. On the morning of December twenty-ninth another search was ordered, during which a scuffle occurred and a shot was fired. The nearly 500 soldiers surrounding the camp opened fire. Hotchkiss guns, rapid-fire, state-of-the-art light artillery of the day, were brought into line. When the firing finally stopped, about 200 Mniconju, including Big Foot, were dead. So ended the Ghost Dance movement and the whole era that white historians call the Indian Wars.

In the years that followed, leaders such as Spotted Tail of the Sicangu and Red Cloud and American Horse of the Oglala counseled that survival necessitated learning to live like the whites. Added to the trauma of unwanted change was the insistence of the U.S. government and its missionary allies that we give up our cultural and ethnic identity. Not only were we to live like the whites, we had to assimilate, or to us, "become white." So began another kind of war, one for the hearts and minds of the generations to come. Yet in spite of the maelstrom of change we had to contend with, we were still viable as far as our tribal identity was concerned, even though books would be written in the twentieth century with titles like *The Last Days of the Sioux Nation*. If my great-grandparents' generation had succumbed to the relentless intent to "kill the Indian and save the man," the battle cry of assimilation voiced by the superintendent of the Carlisle Indian School, the book titles would have been true.

There were no more military conflicts between the Lakota and the United States after 1890. But the period from then to the 1940s was no less fraught with turmoil than the last twenty-five years of the 1800s had been. In 1910 the federal government outlawed the Sun Dance. Whites were allowed to live within the exterior boundaries of the reservations. World War I took many young Lakota men across the ocean to Europe; some of them were conscripted into service, but many volunteered. One of them was my grandfather Charles J. Marshall, who was in the army infantry. I heard him remark one time that he had fought as a mercenary for the United States, which was technically true. Indians weren't granted United States citizenship until 1924 (without asking us if we wanted it, I should add).

Three consequences of white encroachment that all tribes had in common were loss of pre-European lifestyle, loss of land, and loss of culture. The effect was much more devastating on the tribes with smaller populations. The federal government and Christian missionaries knew that the quickest way to destroy a culture is to eliminate its indigenous language. Today, of the nearly 500 tribes still in existence, about 140 retain their native languages. Fortunately, we Lakota are currently one of the five indigenous tribes or nations with the highest percentage of native speakers within our populations—this in spite of intensive and concerted efforts that were the main thrust of the assimilation process.

The Bureau of Indian Affairs and certain churches established boarding schools on the reservations in the early 1900s. Lakota children were placed in the schools and often not allowed to see their parents for the entire school year. There are documented instances where children were not reunited with their parents for several years. Boys with long hair were given haircuts and everyone was expressly forbidden to speak Lakota. Punishment was swift and often severe for anyone who broke the rule. In the 1930s my father was made to kneel on a two-by-four for an entire afternoon the first time he was caught speaking Lakota. The second time he was hung by his thumbs from a basement water pipe and had to stand on tiptoe to avoid dislocating them.

A formal education and Christianity, we were told, was our only salvation because the old days were gone: We could no longer chase buffalo and our spiritual beliefs were heathen and pagan. Much of white society expected us to change our ways and our values like someone taking off one shirt and putting on another. Many of us did embrace Christianity and since we didn't see any buffalo to chase, we changed with the times, and we began to live like anyone else in this country. In spite of the best efforts of Indian agents, teachers, missionaries, and the generally paternalistic mindset of the American public toward all Indians, we still managed to retain enough of our culture and language to keep our identity intact.

Many in my parents' and grandparents' generation don't have a positive opinion about education, which is understandable given the negative experiences they had in the church and government boarding schools, where education was a method of taking away their language and culture. To them anything beyond grammar school or high school was questionable, but in the early 1970s that instrument of forced changed became a way to maintain language and culture.

Education has become a positive, strengthening process because of the wisdom and farsightedness of a few people who felt that Indian-controlled colleges on the reservations were the answer. The first such college was established on the Navajo reservation in 1968 and two Lakota reservations in South Dakota followed suit in 1970 and 1971: Oglala Lakota College on the Pine Ridge Reservation and Sinte Gleska College on the Rosebud Reservation. The primary reason for their establishment is the preservation of language and culture. *Sinte Gleska* is Lakota for Spotted Tail, the last traditional leader of the Sicangu, and the institution named for him is now a four-year university with graduate programs.

There are many challenges besides education that we Lakota need to face as the twenty-first century dawns. Alcoholism continues to be a devastating problem. Legal jurisdiction is another: In the mid 1960s the tribes of South Dakota united to defeat the state's referendum attempt to assume civil and criminal jurisdiction on reservation lands. Loss of land continues to be a challenge and a concern: In 1977 the U.S. Supreme Court upheld the state of South Dakota's contention that four of the five counties comprising the Rosebud Sioux Reservation could no longer be considered reservation because more whites owned land in those counties than members of the tribe. Since then the exterior boundaries of the Rosebud Reservation are the same as for Todd County. Then there is racial prejudice, which in spite of the best efforts from both sides, tends to rear its ugly head occasionally.

All in all we have made significant gains since 1900, but not without some difficulty. In spite of our gains and our losses, we are still Lakota. Lakota language and history is being taught in Indian-controlled schools that were formerly BIA schools, and in a number of public schools as well. The harder the process of assimilation tried to take away our language, our culture, and our identity, the harder we hung on. If the adage mentioned earlier is true—that whatever doesn't kill you will make you stronger—then we are among the sturdiest cultures on the face of the Earth.

Walking the Circle

Kaohomni (ga-oh-ho-mnee), "the circle," is prominent in Lakota life and is used practically and symbolically because it is part of the reality of the physical environment. Toss a stone into a pond and waves flow out from the center in growing circles. A falling leaf in autumn often spins in circles before it lands. The sun and the moon are circular, and from our perspective, they move in circles. The most powerful force on the Plains, the tornado, moves in a circle.

Life itself moves in cycles, or circles. Our annual calendar is a cycle of thirteen months or "moons" because it is based on the cycles of the moon. There are the four seasons that obviously cycle continuously. And the life cycle for all beings is birth, childhood, adulthood, and old age.

A sweat lodge is a simple circular structure that, for me, symbolizes Lakota spiritual beliefs and traditions as well as life itself. The ceremony conducted inside this structure is the *inikagapi,* which doesn't mean sweat lodge nor does it describe any type of structure; it is our word for both the structure and the ceremony. *Inikagapi* means "to make life" or "to renew life." The English interpretation comes from the fact that participants in the ceremony do literally sweat.

The *inikagapi* is a round, totally enclosed structure supported by a framework; imagine half a sphere atop the ground measuring roughly sixteen feet across and four to five feet high at its apex. In the old days the covering was usually buffalo hide; today it is generally canvas. Inside at the very center is a circular pit to hold heated stones. The door usually opens to the east. A ridge of soil a few inches high is formed in a straight line from the edge of the stone pit and ends at the fire pit outside. Outside near the fire pit and in line with it and with the stone pit inside is a stone altar. Sage, a pipe, tobacco, and other items necessary for the ceremony are placed on the altar.

Perhaps the most practical application of the circle was in the design of dwellings. A circular floor plan goes back a long way— so far, in fact that no one can remember when the design was first used. When they lived a semisedentary lifestyle in the forests, our ancestors built dome-shaped, bark- or thatch-covered dwellings. After moving to the Plains, they favored conical hide-covered dwellings. Both could withstand high winds and were relatively easy to erect and take down, and they were built from readily available materials. The conical dwelling or tipi, which means "they live there," was portable as well.

Living in either type of dwelling was a constant reminder for the inhabitants that life flowed in a circle and that they were unalterably connected to everything that was a part of it. So both designs were based on practical as well as spiritual needs.

When my ancestors moved out onto the open Plains, their conical dwellings were arranged in circular encampments as well. A typical encampment, or village, was small—usually twenty to forty families in roughly that many dwellings. When space and topography of a chosen site allowed, a small village would be arranged in a single circular row of dwellings. The larger villages would have double or triple rows of dwellings. Because each individual dwelling faced its door to the east, the entrance to the village was also to the east.

East-facing tipi doors and village entrances were both practical and spiritual: Prevailing winds, especially in autumn and winter, came from the west and northwest, so the door needed to be on the sheltered or lee side of the dwelling. An eastward view was also a greeting to the new sun each day, thereby acknowledging the continuous cycle of life.

One of the most popular designs seen on Lakota art or cultural artifacts is the medicine wheel. The Lakota word for it is *cangleska,* "spotted wood." This literal description is from the four colors painted on the wheel, or hoop, which is made of wood. The shape and the colors used represent the power of life, hence the translated term medicine wheel; having *pejuta* or medicine can mean possessing a certain power or ability.

The medicine wheel is circular with a balanced cross of two intersecting lines in its center; the ends of the lines connect with the wheel at four points. The circle, of course, represents life, and the two intersecting lines represent the two roads in life: the good road, usually painted in red, and the bad road, usually painted black. The good road is also referred to as the Red Road; it is the most difficult to travel. The bad road, the Black, is a wide, easy way to go. These are the two basic choices in life, and we choose one in every situation: the good or the bad. The four sacred colors of red, yellow, black, and white are included in the medicine wheel.

The medicine wheel incorporates another important symbol in Lakota tradition and spirituality: the number four. Like the circle, the number four represents certain realities in life. There are the four seasons—winter, spring, summer, and autumn; the four directions—east, south, west, and north; and the four basic elements of life—Earth, Wind (air), Fire, and Water.

As a symbol or artifact the medicine wheel can be found in two- or three-dimensional Lakota art and in the art of many other tribes as well. It is a sacred or holy symbol for traditional Lakota people, the way the cross is for Christians and the Star of David is for Jews.

The greatest principle the circle symbolizes for me is the equality that applies to all forms of life. In other words, no one form of life is greater or lesser than any other form. We are different from one another certainly, but different is not defined as "greater than" or "less than." And we all share a common journey, the *maka wiconi,* or "life on Earth"—in English, the Circle of Life. This is a much broader scope than the Judeo-Christian ideology that man has dominion over other forms of life. The concept that all life is equal doesn't necessarily circumvent the food-chain viewpoint wherein living things are either prey or predator, those who are eaten and those who do the eating. The smaller, weaker, and slower are killed by the bigger, stronger, and faster. Undeniably that is the way the natural world functions—the survival of the fittest and the strongest, some call it. But whether we are prey or predator, weak or strong, we are all part of a larger community, the largest of all: the Circle of Life.

There is a reality that makes the mole equal to the bear, a reality that connects us all whether we walk, fly, crawl, swim, or grow roots. We are all born and we all die. This is such a simple and quiet reality that we humans allow our arrogance to obscure it and our ignorance to deny it. My maternal grandfather, like many of his generation, was realistic about life and death. He said quite often that death is a part of life. For him death was not a taboo subject to talk about. One of the most profound comments he made provides an insight into the reality that connects all living things. "You cannot fight death," he said, "you can only fight for life."

No matter who and what we are, we are born, more or less fulfill our purpose or destiny, and then we die. The most powerful creature on Earth cannot cheat death. So in that sense the biggest, the swiftest, the most intelligent is no more powerful than the lowliest. In the end the Earth will reclaim us all.

◇◇◇

We don't arrange our dwellings in circles any longer. Our villages are now housing projects and our houses are square; if a front door faces to the east, it most likely isn't intentional. Interestingly, I've noticed that anytime a group of Lakota gather together, they naturally form a circle. Perhaps there is a grain of genetic memory that compels us to subconsciously reconnect with a part of ourselves that has been trampled by television, cyberspace, paternalism, racism, indifference, and other challenges wrought by four generations of cultural upheaval. Though the circle is not as common in everyday life as it once was, it is still a prominent part of our ceremonial lives. Dancing arbors or arenas are round and most of the traditional dances move in a circle—from east to west, of course.

Fortunately, the circle is a never-ending flow, and more young people from each generation are reconnecting with traditions and values. Three years ago I participated in an *inikagapi* where the leader of the ceremony was a young Oglala Lakota in his mid-twenties. A circle, in one sense, continually renews itself. What goes around comes around. For that reason the *inikagapi* is the one ceremony that, for me, represents our cultural rebirth and renewal.

The *inikagapi* ceremony is the process whereby we are able to rediscover ourselves after several generations of confusion. It begins with the outside fire pit, which is usually large and deep; wood and stones are arranged and the fire is lit. The stones are heated until they glow red. At that point the participants are invited into the lodge.

The structure of the sweat lodge represents the womb. We enter it to be reborn. The leader enters first followed by the participants, one by one. The first words that the leader and each participant speaks upon entering the lodge are *mitakuye oyasin,* or "all my relatives." With that simple phrase we connect and align ourselves with all things on and of the Earth, thereby forming a powerful alliance. Each participant circles to the left, in the direction of the sun (or clockwise) and takes a seat. When all are seated, the leader signals the helper, who remains outside, to carry in hot stones and place them in the center pit. A bucket of water is then placed inside, the opening or door is closed and sealed, and there is darkness.

The leader speaks a welcome and provides instructions. He is the first to offer a prayer, acknowledging the Creator, the Earth

Mother, and the powers that live in the Four Directions. There-after each participant offers a prayer as the leader pours water on the hot stones, and the steam fills the space. The temperature rises very quickly in the enclosure and everyone sweats. This is the purification, the purging of one's troubles and the impurities and negativity brought into the lodge. Songs are sung—some as commemorations, some as prayers. When all of the participants have prayed, the leader opens the door and allows a brief respite from the heat. Fresh hot stones are dropped into the pit and the process is repeated. This is done four times. The length of the ceremony depends on the number of participants and the length of their prayers.

When the ceremony inside is concluded the participants exit. The final words they speak as they leave are *mitakuye oyasin*. Their emergence from the lodge or the "womb" symbol-izes their rebirth and a new beginning. Outside they gather in a circle as the leader lights the pipe and each participant is invited to smoke. After that the participants share a meal.

The acknowledgment of the connection to all things living is a real and operative concept for the participants in the cere-mony. Everything that is a part of the ceremony symbolizes that connection, or kinship. The round shape of the lodge rep-resents life itself, and all four elements are part of the ceremony: Earth, Wind (air), Fire, and Water. All the elements and all the relatives—all things living—are brought together to share the bur-dens and give their strength for whatever lies ahead.

Like most participants in an *inikagapi,* I'm reluctant for the ceremony to end, reluctant to leave the warm, comforting em-brace of the womb. Since most ceremonies conclude at night, it isn't unusual to emerge beneath a sky filled with stars, and sometimes with the reassuring presence of the moon as well. The stars and the moon are a constant; they are promises that are never broken and are ever present in our lives as a reminder that life will always flow. They always give me hope.

My grandfather completed his circle on this journey on

March 4, 1975, but he was about to begin another, he told me some months before. "It doesn't end here," he said, "it goes on, in another place, on the other side." Sometimes, especially in winter, when I see a rainbow encircling the sun I imagine that's where he is, somewhere in that circle with my grandmother.

Life goes on, it continues to cycle. The sun comes up each morning and with it comes new opportunity, new hope. No matter what kind of mess I've made of the day before, no matter what victories I've celebrated, each new day is a chance to set the record straight, atone for a mistake, achieve another victory, and take another step on my journey. Each new day is an *inika-gapi,* a chance to be renewed and reborn—another opportunity to be part of the circle that is life, knowing that it is a journey, not a race, and that one doesn't travel it alone.

Index